# Paradise Dammed

## The Tragedy of Lake Turkana

Other titles by the same author:
*Last Man In*
*The Lost Camels of Tartary*
*Shadows across the Sahara*
*The Mysteries of the Gobi*
*Kawndolawa and Itinate: Ritual Pottery of the Cham and Mwana*


For children:
*Rhino's Horn*
*Leopard's Coat*
*Elephant's Tusk*
*The Dragons of Tiananmen Square*
*Letters for a Spy*
*Ticket to Tallinn*
*The Fearless Four*
*The Fearless Four, Hijack!*
*The Fearless Four and the Smugglers*
*The Fearless Four and the Graveyard Ghost*

# Paradise Dammed

## The Tragedy of Lake Turkana

# *John Hare*

Neville & Harding

ISBN: 978-0-948028-10-6 hardback
ISBN: 978-0-948028-11-3 paperback


First published in the UK 2020 by
Neville & Harding
School Farm, Benenden, Kent TN17 4EU

Typeset in Palatino by Helm Information
amandahelm@uwclub.net


Printed and bound in Great Britain by
4Edge Ltd, 22 Eldon Way, Hockley, Essex SS5 4AD
www.4edge.co.uk

*The Team*

For Japper

# Contents

# FOREWORD

## Jane Goodall

When he was a boy, John Hare's father, who lost a leg at the battle of the Somme, told him that obstacles are put in our way to be overcome. And as you read this gripping book, written by a born story-teller, you will marvel at the obstacles that John and his team were able to overcome during their 460-mile expedition around Kenya's Lake Turkana. How proud his father would have been. But as you will find out, the reason for writing the book was not only to recount these sometimes life-threatening experiences, but also to paint a grim picture of paradise lost.

Why is Jane Goodall writing a foreword to a book about an expedition on camels, you may wonder? Well, it all began with a telephone call I received out of the blue in the mid-1990s. A man's voice, on the other end of the line, explained that he was John Hare, and that his wife's aunt had known my mother since the 1930s. And as the story unfolded I found that the aunt was none other than my godmother, and that I had known John's wife when she was a little girl!

Once we had sorted out this somewhat amazing connection, John got down to the real reason he was calling. He had become passionately involved in an effort to save the critically endangered wild double-humped camel in Mongolia and in China's remote Gobi Desert which was formerly a nuclear test site. As he told me about his mission I became increasingly fascinated and wanted to know more. We arranged to meet for lunch, and by the end of two hours John had persuaded me to become the Life Patron of his newly established UK charity, the Wild Camel Protection Foundation. We had also laid the grounds for a friendship that has only grown stronger over the years. We discovered we had certain things in common. When I was a ten-year-old I decided that when I grew up I would go to Africa and live with wild animals and write books about them. When John was a twelve-year-old, and his father asked him what he wanted to be when he grew up, he answered without hesitation, "I want to be an explorer." History has proved that we both followed our dreams and we both succeeded in making those dreams reality. And yet we realised our dreams in environments that could not be more different: for me in the rain forest, for John in waterless deserts.

In a way I also became an explorer, starting my study of wild chimpanzees in an area of Tanzania that was remote and relatively unknown back in 1960. But whereas my exploration revealed previously unknown aspects of the behaviour of one species, the chimpanzee, in one location, Gombe National Park, John's zest for exploration led him to make discoveries of previously unknown places in some of the wildest and most remote regions of the planet.

An early adventure took him to the Mandara Mountains along the Nigeria/Cameroun border in West Africa when he was working for the British Government. And there he actually discovered an isolated, hidden village, which had escaped the attention of all the government authorities and had never before been mapped.

His second discovery was years later when, during one of his expeditions in China to learn about the range of the wild camels in the Desert of Lop, he and his team of Chinese scientists discovered, deep in sand dunes, a fresh water spring in that salt water desert that is two-third the size of France. This spring had trapped and sustained what scientists call, "a naïve population of wild life" – wild animals that had never, ever seen man and subsequently behaved as if, John says, "that extraordinary, upright, two-legged (and two-faced) creature was of no consequence whatsoever."

During one of our irregular meetings John told me that he began his work with the wild camels of the Gobi as "a romantic, idealistic explorer" and his involvement with them had come about through a series of coincidences. Coincidences which enabled him to become the first foreigner in 45 years to enter China's former nuclear test area. One thing led to another, and in 1997 he co-founded the Wild Camel Protection Foundation which established, in the Desert of Lop, one of the largest nature reserves in the world. I remember helping him to raise funds for one of the ranger posts.

At that time, having seen how these amazing camels survived in that most hostile of environments and learned how close they were to becoming extinct, he morphed from an idealistic explorer into a passionate conservationist, dedicated to protecting and saving this little-known species. Just as I morphed from a researcher into an activist when I realized how fast chimpanzee numbers were decreasing in the wild.

John was able to attract many high-profile supporters and this, along with his ability as a raconteur, was gradually raising awareness among the general public about the plight of the wild camel. But he also needed, increasingly, to raise funds and it was to get added publicity and attract new donors that he undertook the incredibly challenging expedition described in this book, an expedition that often put him and his team in great danger.

His plan was to circumambulate the whole of Lake Turkana, situated in the wild, remote and inhospitable lands of northern Kenya. One of the few ways of getting around is with camels – the one-humped dromedary species. Such a trek had never before been attempted mainly because of the camels' inability to cross the mighty Omo River, which flows out of the highlands of Ethiopia and is two football pitches wide – and full of crocodiles. It was the danger that appealed to John, of course! In 2006, 60 years after he announced his desire to be an explorer, that passion was still alive in the 72-year-old man. And when you read this book you will probably be astounded, as I was, that John, as well as his whole team, survived!

Eight Kenyans accompanied him, six Africans and two Europeans, and all (except him) under the age of thirty-five. "They were wonderful people," he told me. Indeed they must have been! They accomplished their goal and they survived – and this despite being held up by Turkana tribesmen with Kalashnikovs and despite having travelled in temperatures which were frequently over 50° Celsius and on one notable occasion in the Suguta valley south of Lake Turkana reached 60.1° Celsius on Josh Perrett's chronometer.

Yet after he returned from that expedition, John told me he did not think the story would make a book! Of course I disagreed with him, but his mind was made up.

Fourteen years after that expedition, during another of our meetings, John told me that a book would be written after all. Not just about his amazing adventure, but about the calamitous situation that has arisen in the Omo Delta since. He told me that five huge dams had been built on the Omo River. The Dassenech people who live in the Delta and who had helped to transport the team's camels across the Omo, had been cruelly evicted from their ancestral homes. And it had been the same for other tribes whose lands embraced the river to the north. Today they are no longer able to farm in the way their forebears farmed for millennia.

And that means that centuries of collective wisdom relating to livestock, bi-annual flood-dependent cultivation, and complex tribal agricultural practices that were in harmony with the environment, have been ruthlessly obliterated. And it is not only the Omo Delta and the Omo riverine area in Ethiopia that have been affected – Lake Turkana's water level has fallen dramatically and the 100,000 people who live around or near the lake are now short of food.

And there is one more tragic outcome. As a result of the work of the Leakey family and other paleontologists, excavations in the Lake Turkana area have contributed greatly to our understanding of human evolution. The area to the west and to the east of the lake, now known as the Cradle of Mankind, was a geological trap which, when excavated, provided a glimpse into the lives of the earliest humans. But the current developments in the Omo Delta, which have shattered the stability of the lake, puts the future of our Cradle in grave danger.

Why were these dams built, at vast expense? Because the Ethiopian government is transforming more than 926,000 acres of the lower Omo River into industrial plantations. Vast areas of land adjacent to the west bank of the Omo River have been designated for growing sugar and cotton.

John Hare is fully aware that indigenous peoples cannot be kept for ever locked in a time warp that prohibits development. He knows that progress is inevitable. But he feels strongly that great changes in life styles should be introduced humanely and in collaboration with the local communities, not by using force on peoples who have successfully survived in the area for thousands of years.

The people of the Omo and its Delta, like the wild camels in China and Mongolia, are now critically endangered. Their voice has been silenced. The second half of this inspiring book gives them a voice.

Jane Goodall

*Lieutenant Ritter Ludwig von Höhnel, a member of Count Sámuel
Teleki von Szék's expedition, looking out in wonder towards Lake
Turkana over Porr Hill on 5th March 1888.
They were the first Europeans to discover the lake.*

# 1

# The Background

Taking camels around Lake Turkana in northern Kenya was never going to be easy.

The biggest and most obvious obstacle to a journey around Turkana, is the Omo (Nianam) River, flowing southwards from the Ethiopian highlands into this most northern of eight Rift Valley lakes; the river is wider than two football pitches and flush with Nile crocodiles *(Crocodylus niloticus)*. It is little wonder there is no known record of camels having previously crossed the Omo.

Then there is the Loriu Plateau which rises to nearly 5,000 feet, on the western shore, south of where the Kerio River flows into the lake. Up to this point, it is possible to walk almost along the whole of the sandy shoreline to the east and west of the lake, but the Loriu Plateau's sheer slopes plunge directly into the lake's waters and can only be crossed by going over the top, a lengthy expanse covered in lava and abhorrent to camels. Camels' feet are fashioned for desert and sand, not for razor-sharp, brittle, unpredictable lava.

I had found no record of camels having been taken across the Omo River and over the top of Loriu, which explained why in recorded history Lake Turkana has not been circumambulated by explorers and travellers using these remarkable creatures.

Lake Turkana is the world's largest permanent desert lake

and the world's largest alkaline lake. By volume it is the world's fourth-largest salt-water lake after the Caspian Sea, Issyk Kul in the Tien Shan mountains of Kyrgyzstan, and Turkey's Lake Van.

One other factor complicated the journey. Severe drought in the Horn of Africa had caused the Turkana and the Gabbra tribes to fight for valuable grazing land that the Turkana had in recent years been using along the eastern shore. The Turkana had crossed from the western side of the lake in sturdy boats, donated by missionaries to help the tribesmen to catch the sometimes two-metre long Nile perch (*Lates niloticus*). These kind people had no idea their generosity would enable the Turkana to wage marine warfare. People were fleeing their homes, cattle, sheep and goats were being rustled, and men were being slaughtered, but not by spears, bows and arrows. The warriors carried the brainchild of Lieutenant-General Mikhail Timofeyevich Kalashnikov – the AK47.

A trip like this requires planning and cash. Plans had been made. Cash had been raised. We had all agreed we were not going to cancel our attempt to make the journey just because there was bad blood between the tribes.

The team comprised 25-year-old Josh Perrett, grandson of my good friend the late Jasper Evans; Ivan Jensen, like Josh also in his twenties; and 71-year-old me. I am not one ever to contemplate failure and I was taught by my father and have always believed that obstacles are put in our way to be overcome.

But I knew I could not walk around the lake. My plus three score years and ten would see to that. Josh and Ivan would trek around without a problem, but I would have to ride. Not that riding a camel presented any difficulty. I had crossed the Sahara on the back of a camel and undertaken numerous camel treks in the harsh Gobi Desert of China and Mongolia. My only concern was that I would hold the others up.

The eighteen dromedary camels we took with us all came from Jasper's ranch, Ol Maisor, near Rumuruti on Kenya's Laikipia Plateau. Jasper was devoted to camels, was extremely knowledgeable about them and kept a herd of over 200. He had co-authored the manual, *Camel Keeping in Kenya* (1994) and there was very little he did not know about every aspect of managing domestic dromedaries in Africa. During the 1990s he had travelled to Pakistan to buy sturdy and thick-set, single-humped Pakistani dromedaries to cross with his native Kenyan and Somali dromedaries to increase their milk yield. This project had been a great success and resulted in camels with teats "like Coca Cola bottles" – to quote Jasper.

Of course, Jasper's dromedaries were very different from the double-humped wild camel (*Camelus ferus*), which the Wild Camel Protection Foundation was endeavouring to save from extinction in the Gobi Desert, but they were all part of the same camelid family. Camelids are members of the biological family *Camelidae*. The extant members of this group are: wild double-humped camels, dromedary camels, Bactrian camels, llamas, alpacas, vicuñas, and guanacos, and they all originated millions of years ago in the Arizona Desert in America. And for me there was an overriding reason to undertake the journey. The double-humped and critically endangered wild camel which lives in the Chinese and Mongolian Gobi Desert had just been declared by scientists a new and separate species of camel, which had separated from any other known form of camel over 750,000 years ago. I had been researching the wild camel for the past thirteen years and this was the news our British charity, the Wild Camel Protection Foundation (WCPF), had been anxiously waiting to hear.

The WCPF had part-funded Dr Pamela Burger, a senior genetic scientist at the Veterinary University in Vienna, to undertake genetic tests on wild camel samples collected from the Gobi Desert in China and Mongolia over the previous five years. I was anxious that this sensational news should be circulated as widely as possible and the Lake Turkana expedition, using single-humped dromedary camels bred in Kenya and the publicity it would raise, was a wonderful means of achieving this.

Aside from Josh and Ivan the hard core of the team were the six camel herdsmen recruited from Ol Maisor. The roll call of these men reads like a combined list of Tolkien and Biblical characters:

Barabara, Lerebaiyan, Epekor, Surbey, Moses, Kamau.

Of different tribal backgrounds they had been carefully chosen by Josh. Some were the sons or even grandsons of men who had worked for Jasper in the past. Josh had grown up with many of the younger ones and played with them as a boy. But familiarity had not bred contempt and although Josh frequently spoke to them as an equal, he never once lost his underlying authority. His spoken Swahili was fluent and in the evening, sitting around the campfire he would talk to them on any subject from sex to rap but never once amidst the banter was he shown the slightest disrespect.

Only some spoke English; my African languages, Hausa and Fulani, took me a long way in West Africa but in East Africa they were of no use whatsoever. And my feeble Swahili was limited to kitchen talk. As in any human grouping, there were extroverts and introverts, clowns, jesters and men of few words and deep thoughts. But they had put aside their tribal differences and had welded into a team who would follow Josh to the ends of the earth.

They reminded me of the detribalised African carriers who used to head load my kit on countless treks in Northern Nigeria. Scallywags and rascals when they arrived, their respect had to be earned. But once you had earned it and remained scrupulously fair in your dealings with them, they would trek on with you forever.

They, together with the 18 Ol Maisor dromedary camels, were what we relied on to take us on the 460-mile journey around the lake. And not one of them, man or beast, would let us down.

Our food and kit were carried in twelve long wooden boxes, two strapped on either side of a camel. Jasper who devised these camel boxes had fashioned some of them with lids, which could be swivelled into a 45° position and used as a table. As we were setting out around Lake Turkana at the beginning of the rainy season, it was essential our food supplies and kit had good protection from both sun and rain.

During my seven years trekking in Northern Nigeria I survived on a Spartan diet. One remote region where I worked, the Mambilla Plateau, which on its eastern side is contiguous with the Cameroun border, did not have any road access and anything imported had to be loaded on to carriers' heads and carried 5,000 feet up the steep sides of the plateau.

And during a three-and-a-half month trek across the Sahara with Jasper, we survived on a no-frills diet. Apart from the essentials of tea, sugar, tinned milk, tinned margarine – and whisky – it was spam, corned beef and tinned fish. Fresh fruit and vegetables soon withered in the heat and only onions and, surprisingly, cabbages kept for any length of time. Cabbages would turn a slimy black but when cut in half their hearts were invariably green and fresh.

For meat, apart from the tinned bully beef and spam, we ate dried goat or sheep when we could get it. Pasta was the staple not rice, which is too water dependent. Dried peppers added spice to a dull meal and dates kept one healthy and regular.

Whenever I see food in shops today with a sell-by date stamped on the packet, I think of what I ate on my desert journeys and on Mambilla. It grieves me to see the amount of perfectly good and edible food which is wasted because of a "past its sell-by date" directive.

My much younger companions were certainly not prepared to travel around the lake on a frugal diet. I was amazed at the tins of fruit and packets of cheese, chocolate and other luxuries – including tinned camel goulash made by Josh's father – that were stowed neatly in the camel boxes. Not that I complained – far from it.

On Mambilla, my cook Luttu could turn out delicious bread cooked in two empty kerosene tins with a fire between them and a piece of expanded metal lying over the flames and balanced on the sides of the tins. We did not rise to the giddy heights of bread-making during our trek – but we ate well.

Jasper drove me the 300 miles from his ranch to a small bay on the lake – Sandy Bay – near the dry riverbed of the Sirima Lugga watercourse. Josh, Ivan and the camel boys had already brought the camels on foot from the ranch, through the notoriously tough and difficult Suguta Valley, one of the hottest regions in East Africa where temperatures can reach over 60° Celsius.

At the north end of the Suguta they had had to get round a small salt lake called Logipi which is surrounded by treacherous hot, mud springs. They were then faced with an ancient lava barrier to cross before they reached the southernmost tip of Lake Turkana. But that was not the end. There was a final obstacle, a vast, brittle, field of lava, which had flowed 100 years earlier into the lake from an active volcano named after the Hungarian explorer Count Teleki (1845–1916). All this in temperatures, which at one point reached 60.1° Celsius – and this before the real journey had even begun.

On one occasion, Kasungu, their white tail-end camel, slipped into one of the hot streams, which flow under encrusted soda at the Lorusio hot springs, near Karpedo. The crust broke and before they were able to roll, push and pull Kasungu out he was severely burned. The team staggered into their camp that evening, blistered and exhausted.

Next day, they started at 2.00 a.m. and covered approximately 20 miles before 9.00 a.m., when the heat forced them to call a halt. Turkana tribesmen directed Josh to a source of sweet water near a small waterfall on the bank of the Suguta. The Turkana warned them not to swim in the pool, as reputedly there was both a crocodile and a python living there. Good advice that was ignored. That evening a five-foot crocodile rushed at one of the men as he tried to collect a bucketful of water. He just managed to scramble back up the bank in time.

Two friends who were accompanying them had had to give up before completing the Suguta trek. In past years, it was alleged that battle-hardened SAS troops on a training exercise had collapsed in Suguta heat. I had completed the northern half of the Suguta Valley with camels nine years earlier but had ended the trek at the southern end of Lake Turkana. Josh, Ivan, the camel men and the camels had reached the lake after an extremely arduous trek, but had an even tougher journey ahead of them.

I first met Josh, the son of Jasper's daughter, Amanda, and son-in-law, John Perrett, as a 13-year-old when he was poking about in his grandfather's workshop explaining the mysteries of a caterpillar to the astonishment of his two younger sisters. Clean cut and well put together, I immediately warmed to him. When he was twenty I asked his parents if he would be able to come with his grandfather when we crossed the Sahara with camels but his parents had felt that risking the life of one member of the family was quite enough.

Above all he had that rarest and most precious of qualities, so valuable in the African bush as elsewhere in life – common sense – an attribute which outweighs any amount of book learning. A professional hunter in Tanzania, he had a deep knowledge of bush craft and like his grandfather Jasper was quick to act when he saw anyone, black or white, in potential difficulty or trouble.

His good friend Ivan had many of these qualities too, but was more introspective. Thoughtful and precise, he was an excellent amateur vet for the camels, which later in the journey was a skill they sorely needed – especially when crossing the lava fields.

Both Ivan and Josh had girlfriends; Josh's girlfriend Donna was Ivan's sister, they talked about the girls so incessantly that I felt at the end of the journey I knew them intimately. Donna was a member of the Suguta Valley team and had distinguished herself by trekking all the way up the valley in flip-flops. By the end of the trek her feet were completely taped up with sticking plaster to ward off the heat of the Suguta sand. Josh subsequently married Donna.

I felt we had a great team and was confident we would succeed in our objective but I sensed Jasper was not quite so sure I would complete the arduous journey.

Stephen Pern, an ex-officer from the Parachute Regiment, had completed an extraordinary trek around the lake with three donkeys in the late 1970s, so in this respect our expedition was not a 'first' – but it was a 'first' for a traveller with camels.

Pern had another extraordinary 'first' which I definitely did not attempt to emulate. He reveals in his book about his journey around the lake, *Another Land, Another Sea* (1979) the following:

> That night I drank my first bowl of blood. It had been brought over
> from the next *manyatta* [compound] and was slightly congealed,
> but Orip, daughter of the house, had kept it for me. She mixed
> in a little milk and offered it to me with a grin. I sealed off my
> sensibilities and shut my eyes. It slid down my throat in a rush
> and I was wiping my beard, smiling and saying how good it was. I
> did not mind it at all really, but I did find the soup Orip had made
> pretty nauseating. Pieces of offal were cut and boiled together
> with the goat's chopped but unwashed stomach. The result was a
> hot green morass with oily blobs floating in the steam.

I have long admired men and women who journey alone
with only locals for company. Pern completed his pioneering
journey with two Turkana men and showed quite remarkable
resourcefulness and resilience. It is a great tale of African travel,
which has not been given the full credit due.

Lake Turkana, which was called Rudolf during the colonial
era, has had many African names, *The Sea of Many Fish* by the
Turkana and in the *Geographical Journal* of 1894 it was referred to
as *Basso Narok*, the Black Lake in the Samburu language. It is 154
miles from north to south and while the water is safe to drink
although very alkaline, one's stomach objects if it is drunk over a
lengthy period.

It is called the Jade Sea because of its striking turquoise colour,
caused by the algae, and algae surface blooms, making it a major
stopover for migrating waterfowl. The lake has many native fish,
cichlids and barb and a number of introduced fish including
the Nile tilapia (*Oreochromis niloticus*) and Nile perch. Its central
and southern volcanic islands are a breeding ground for Nile
crocodiles. It harbours hippos and a multitude of venomous
snakes and scorpions. When the first explorers discovered the
lake, they encountered hundreds of elephants and rhinos but
these have now completely disappeared. The frequent use of the
word Nile suggests correctly an historic connection to the Nile
River and the Nile River Basin.

Rocky outcrops are found on the east and south shores of the lake, while dunes, spits and flats are on the west and north, at a lower elevation. On-shore and off-shore winds can be extremely strong, as the lake warms and cools more slowly than the land. Sudden, violent storms are frequent and a novice in a boat on the lake can quickly and unexpectedly find himself in real difficulty – as can a light aircraft caught in volatile winds.

In the 1930s George Adamson, husband of Joy of *Born Free* fame, future game warden and lover of lions, but at that time a penniless prospector for gold, made an unorthodox crossing of Lake Turkana with two companions. Reluctant to trek from one side of the lake to the other, they built a coracle out of acacia timber, none of which was straight. They bound it together with thongs and strips of rawhide and covered it with tarpaulin. When the hull was ready they made two crude oars from acacia poles bound to donkey boxes as paddles and fashioned their bedrolls into a makeshift sail. The night before they were due to set off, their boat was damaged in the night by a strong wind and hyenas ate the leather rawhide thongs. Undeterred, they started construction all over again. When they finally launched at 3.00 p.m. in the afternoon two days later, it was clear that the wind was too strong for the sail so they decided to row across the 12-mile wide lake.

The two oarsman, their hands blistered and bleeding and with their African companion continuously baling out water, judged that at dusk they were half-way across the lake. There was no moon and they were unable to see where they were going. They eventually landed on the other side of the lake in the middle of the night, guided to their mooring by the distinctive croaking of a multitude of frogs, which they had at first thought was the sound of an approaching storm. Half an hour after they had landed a gale blew like fury for the remainder of the night until late next morning. Had it caught them on the lake the boat could not have survived for more than a few minutes.

Three rivers, the Omo, the Turkwell and the Kerio, flow into the lake but lacking an outflow its only water loss is by evaporation and this concentrates the carbonate salts. Lake volume and dimensions are variable. For example, its level fell by eleven yards between 1975 and 1993. Due to temperature, aridity and geographic inaccessibility, the lake retains its wild and unpredictable character. An abundance of hominid fossils have been discovered in the area surrounding Lake Turkana.

The name Rudolf was given to the lake when the wealthy Hungarian aristocrat, Count Sámuel Teleki von Szék, discovered it for the world and named it after his friend and patron, Crown Prince Rudolf of Austria.

*Count Sámuel Teleki von Szék*

An adventurous and resolute man, Teleki was an excellent shot, an accomplished mountaineer and a tireless traveller who made a pioneering two-year expedition of discovery across East Africa with over 280 porters. He also fearlessly spoke his mind. On one occasion while discussing the inaccuracies and exaggerations of earlier African explorers, someone said that he hoped that he would stick to the facts when he wrote his book on his travels. He retorted, "My dear, Sir, all African travellers are liars, my old friend Burton was a liar, Speke and Grant were liars, Stanley is a liar, we know our friends Thompson and Johnston are liars, and" (with a slight bow and patting his brick-red chest) "I am going to be a liar. If I do not discover a lake I shall say I did; if I do not discover a mountain I shall say I did; and who will disprove it until long after I receive the credit?"

Nicknamed Bwana Tumbo (Mr. Belly) on account of his portly figure, the epithet must have been inappropriate, for by the end of his arduous journey he had lost five stone (32 kilos) and at one point had been close to starvation. A confirmed bachelor, he was also eccentric in his dress. He always wore his shirt wide open, shaved his already nearly bald head, never wore a jacket and constantly smoked his long-stemmed German pipe.

His flamboyant nature and style can be gleaned from a letter he wrote to his patron, Prince Rudolf while he was getting his expedition together in Zanzibar.

> For two months now I have been inhaling the garlic-scented sweat of the blacks who pack, lift, move and weigh our goods in my store, day after day, amid infernal noise. Such "mesigos" [loads], some 450 of them, are needed to satisfy the greed of the Maasai and Kikuyu and the demands of my porters' bellies. A happy land is this, everything grows here except mokka [coffee] and that is hard to come by. It is full of the worst type of European swindlers, fraudulent big merchants, missionaries turned into head-waiters, French black nuns given to coquetry, scientific researchers who cannot count! A European hotel with a black poison-monger and, I may add, nourishment to which one truly needs to become acclimatised, as I have.

My hotel is very good – it is four weeks since the window broke, and in pours the rain! The chair is mine and it is my Somali and negro servants who serve the whole hotel. Incidentally everyone is cheerful here. If you talk to someone he promptly runs off to do you a favour, never extends his hand and is amazed if he is given something. The virgins hail you with loud "Jambos" [hello] and open their mouths wide enough for a coconut. My good friend, the Sultan [of Zanzibar], is original in his outlook. The Germans try to skin him, the English won't allow it so that they in turn may skin him quietly later. The one is rude to him, infinitely tactless and bullying; the other protects him, spoils him, fills him with money but has the same aim – to take the skin off him. You will guess who manages better.

In great contrast, his white companion on his arduous trek was an Austrian from a middle-class family called Lieutenant Ritter Ludwig von Höhnel. Thirteen years Teleki's junior, his character was completely different. Where Teleki was flamboyant, extrovert and adventurous, von Höhnel was precise, methodical and cautious. He had a remarkable ability to observe and record what he saw with exemplary accuracy, despite frequent debilitating setbacks from disease and hunger. At the end of their long journey of discovery, it was von Höhnel who produced the remarkably graphic two volumes of record of their journey entitled *Discovery of Lakes Rudolf and Stephanie.*

In the book, he describes his reaction to his first sight of the lake. So little had changed, that when we made our journey in 2006 apart from there being a road to the lake from the south, this description of the lake's discovery in March 1888 could have been recorded in the same manner.

Teleki's and von Höhnel's great moment came on an intensely hot afternoon in March – the hottest month of the year. It was a momentous day for the two men who had endured the anguish and enjoyed the pleasures of travelling in Africa for thirteen months. But before reaching the lake and with no certain knowledge that there was a lake ahead of them, von Höhnel initially paints a dismal picture:

*Lieutenant Ritter Ludwig von Höhnel*

No living creature shared the solitude with us, and as far as our glass could reach there was nothing to be seen but desert, desert everywhere. To all this was added the scorching heat and the ceaseless buffeting of the sand-laden wind against which we were powerless to protect ourselves.

Later:

The scenery became more and more dreary as we advanced. The barren ground was strewn with gleaming, chiefly red and green volcanic debris, pumice stone, huge blocks of blistered lava, and here and there pieces of petrified wood. There was no regular path and we had to pick our way carefully among the scoriae, some of which was as sharp as knives.

He then continued:

Steep rocky slopes alternated with ravines strewn with debris, which gave one the impression of being still glowing hot and of having been flung forth from some huge forge. And the glaring monotony continued till about two o'clock. The good spirits with which the thought that we were nearing the end of our long tramp had filled us in the morning had long since dissipated . . . when all of a sudden, as we were climbing a gentle slope, such a grand, beautiful and far reaching scene was spread out before us, that at first we felt we must be under delusion and were disposed to think the whole thing a mere phantasmagoria as we got higher up, a single peak gradually rose before us, the gentle contours rising symmetrically from every side, resolving themselves into one broad pyramid mountain, which we knew at once to be a volcano. A moment before we had been gazing into empty space, and now here was a mighty mountain mass looming up before us, on the summit of which we almost involuntarily looked for snow. This was, however only the result of an optical delusion caused by the suddenness with which the mountain had come into sight, and from the fact that the land sank rapidly on either side of it, whilst we were gazing up at it from a considerable height. On the east side of the mountain the land was uniformly flat, a golden plain lit up by sunshine, whilst on the west the base of the volcano seemed to rise up out of a bottomless depth, a void which was altogether a mystery to us. We hurried as fast as we could to the top of the ridge, the scene gradually developing itself as we advanced, until an entirely new world was spread out before our astonished eyes. The void down in the depths beneath us became filled as if by magic with picturesque mountains and rugged slopes, with a medley of ravines and valleys, which appeared to be closing up from every side to form a fitting frame for the dark-blue gleaming surface of the lake stretching away beyond as far as the eye could reach.

For a long time we gazed in speechless delight, spell-bound by the beauty of the scene before us, whilst our men equally silent, stared into the distance for a few minutes, to break presently into shouts of astonishment at the sight of the glittering expanse of the great lake, which melted on the horizon into the blue of the sky. At that moment all our danger, all our fatigues were forgotten in the joy of finding our exploring expedition crowned with success at last.

The date was 5th March 1888. Von Höhnel then went on to describe the naming of this dark-blue gleaming lake:

Full of enthusiasm and gratefully remembering the gracious interest taken in our plans from the first by his Royal and Imperial Highness, Prince Rudolf of Austria, Count Teleki named the sheet of water, set like a pearl of great price in the wonderful landscape beneath us – Lake Rudolf.

Von Höhnel was directly responsible for the route of the expedition, which led to this discovery. Teleki had wanted the expedition to head south towards today's Tanzania where among other plans he would hunt and climb to the summit of the hitherto unconquered Mount Kilimanjaro. He was to take with him his trusty, old friend Baron Arz, a companion on previous African hunting trips. But the expedition's patron intervened and introduced him to the young Austrian naval lieutenant, Ludwig von Höhnel. Prince Rudolf wanted von Höhnel to travel with Teleki instead of Baron Arz. Although Teleki's junior in rank, age and class, von Höhnel forcibly suggested the expedition should head north into unexplored territory instead of hunting in discovered land to the south – and Prince Rudolf supported him. Teleki, in deference to his patron's wishes, was forced to drop his desired companion and to agree to the expedition's change of plan.

One can but sympathise with Teleki at that stage. His private arrangements had been thwarted by the Crown Prince's interference, and instead of the pleasant companionship of an old friend, he had been encumbered with an upstart who was responsible for diverting him from his original plan. For this reason, Teleki adopted a cool off-hand manner to von Höhnel throughout the expedition. Nevertheless, he did recognise his sterling qualities and in a letter to Prince Rudolf wrote that:

> Höhnel is a very knowledgeable man, a good fellow, we never clash over anything, moreover he is clever and brave.

How ironic that Rudolf's memorial, until it was renamed Turkana, was the spectacular Jade Sea situated in a remote part of Africa and that another lake to the northeast, also discovered by Teleki, was named after his cold and unfeeling wife, Stephanie. But the lake's former naming after the depressive Rudolf is, in 2020, highly appropriate: 140 years later the lake, the jewel among all the Rift Valley lakes, is being deliberately destroyed by a gigantic construction. Depression, hunger and despair, as will become clear later in this book, are stalking Lake Turkana's rapidly receding shoreline.

The area has always been harsh, and unforgiving. Since their beginnings, the tribes around Lake Turkana have shifted, fought one another, mingled, been ejected or even adopted by their enemies. The modern world has brought roads and transport but no wealth and prosperity. But nothing can be done to control the vagaries of nature and the climate, and near the lake the biblical seven lean years come with an increasing frequency accelerated by climate change. As a consequence survival techniques are a way of life for those living in this extremely hostile yet starkly beautiful part of Africa.

The nineteenth century saw huge turmoil, the tribes fighting continuously through the early decades.

And in the last two decades of that century the nomads' precarious existence was further aggravated by immense disasters. Pernicious diseases reduced the human population and their cattle were cut down by *rinderpest*, a cattle disease which accompanied the arrival of the white man. This coupled with marauding bands from Ethiopia encouraged by the ruthless Emperor Menelik made for huge hardship and deprivation. But

*Emperor*
*Menelik*

the really significant year was 1888 when the first white man arrived at the lake.

After over 60 years of trying, even the British could not completely control the Turkana tribe and the Kenya government does not have total control over them today. In the nineteenth century they developed into a formidable and aggressive force and took complete control of the territory on the western side of the lake and some on the east. They chased the Dassanech into the Omo Delta to the north and the Samburu to the south. Tall, lean, dark-skinned, tough as iron and utterly ruthless, they pillaged and sacked the encampments of neighbouring tribes, fought to enlarge their territory and plundered and murdered their way to supremacy. Tribal elders sanction these raids, as cattle are the tribal currency. Without cattle a man can neither marry nor hold an honoured position within the tribe. Their womenfolk encourage them to go on a raid since without surplus cattle they are unlikely ever to acquire a husband.

A man can live with a girl and have children by her until he can acquire enough cattle to buy her or until another man comes along and buys her at a reduced price. If another man buys her, he buys her children as well and the boys become his sons and herdsmen. If girls, they are accepted as his daughters and eventually sold off into marriage. But for the boys to make any headway at all, they have to acquire cattle. The only way to do this is to go on a raid and steal them.

Pressure to go on a raid, therefore, comes from many directions. It is the one route to stability and success within the tribe. Raids to increase the size of their herds are even today considered quite normal practice.

A British army officer posted near Lake Turkana recorded a conversation with a Turkana chieftain in the 1950s, which dramatically portrays the Turkana mind-set on raiding neighbouring tribes.

> "Chaggi, you have the scars for women victims as well as men victims; have you killed many?"
>
> "Effendi, I have killed a great many. I have few scars; there would be no room for them all if I put one for every one of our enemies, the Suk, that I have killed."

[Suk meaning snot, is an insulting name for the Pokot, who live further south of the lake, remaining historically aloof from outside influences. They dwell not in villages but in family groups in huts, scattered around small clearings in the acacia woodland.]

> "Tell me, Chaggi, when you raid the Suk do you lead out a large army of spearmen?"
>
> "Effendi, I often raid alone. I go over the border with no one else at all. I reach a *manyatta* [hut] as day is about to dawn; I kill everyone there and then I go home with the cattle. It is the custom of our tribe to raid for cattle and that has been the custom always."
>
> "What glory is there, Chaggi, in killing women?"
>
> "It isn't glory, it's sense."
>
> "So you deliberately kill women, Chaggi?"
>
> "And children too."
>
> "Have you no use for women as wives?"
>
> "Effendi, I am a Turkana. The Turkana like Turkana girls as

wives. I do not want Suk women. I do not want a wife who is grieving over the husband whom I have killed."

"Why don't you just let the women go, Chaggi?"

"Do you know anything about women, Effendi?"

"Not much, I am hoping you will tell me."

"Effendi, women are the ones to make trouble. If I raid for cattle and kill all the men and let all the women go, the women run off screaming until they find some more men, and then they so disturb the hearts of these men that the men set out on a raid to get back all the cattle again. That is why I run after the women and push a spear into them. It is just a matter of sense; no Turkana thinks it a glory to kill a woman."

"And then about the very small children – do you even spear them?"

"Effendi, what do you expect, little children need mothers and milk to keep them alive. When their cattle have gone with me taking their milk with them and when the others are lying dead, what is there for the little children to look forward to except a hyena?"

"So then, Chaggi, once you pick on a Suk manyatta, you kill everyone in it, even to the babes that can neither speak nor walk."

"Certainly, 'Kluch'." (sound of spear penetrating).

Jasper Evans, who employed over 150 Kenyans on Ol Maisor, admired the Turkana as the toughest of the tough for whom no job was too difficult, no journey too taxing. The women he found were equal to their menfolk in their resilience to hardship.

In times of drought the Turkana will slit carefully around a camel's hump and scoop out fat for personal nourishment before sewing the skin flap back again. On their wrists they still wear a wrist knife, its razor-sharp blade ever ready to slash the face of an opponent. And all this violent activity in a land where temperatures frequently hover near 50° Celsius.

Camels, whether double-humped Bactrians or single-humped dromedaries, are the most extraordinarily well-designed animals for the harshest desert environment. In lush, green pastures or confined behind bars in a zoo, camels look completely out of place. But in a dry, cold or hot desert they are totally in their element.

Unfortunately, among the unknowing they have a bad reputation. It is alleged they are capable of kicking out with all four feet, can give a particularly nasty bite with their yellow teeth and are capable of blowing undigested food all over an irritant, be he man or beast. In addition, they have bad breath. Camels are indeed capable of displaying all these traits, but as with horses and indeed all domestic animals, there are the good and the bad, the ill-tempered and the docile, and their positives far outweigh their negatives.

When hungry, a camel can eat almost anything – old leather, rope, a cast-off shoe. The inside of its mouth can cope with needle sharp, six-inch thorns from acacia trees, cactus spines or even bones and splinters of wood. But it is not destructive of its environment like sheep or goats, which pull up grass by the roots and speed up the process of soil erosion and desertification. A camel in the main browses on shrubs and bushes, many of which have a wonderful protective mechanism. The camel can bite off and chew the branch until it reaches a section which tastes extremely bitter. It will then jerk its head away – saving the bush from complete destruction.

Camel humps are filled with fat, not water as many people believe, and a full dromedary's single hump can hold up to 80 pounds of fat. During periods when a camel is unable to browse for food, it draws on this emergency food supply, the fat automatically seeping into its body from the hump. A camel can go for up to thirteen days when carrying loads – sometimes weighing as much as 400 pounds – without having to drink. When grazing contentedly on its own, he can last for a month without water.

How does a camel achieve this remarkable feat? A camel has been known to drink 27 gallons of water in ten minutes. This huge amount of liquid first enters its stomach and then a myriad of blood vessels absorb and carry the water to every part of its body. It has been discovered that a camel's stomach can empty itself of 20 gallons of water in ten minutes. After drinking this prodigious quantity the camel not unnaturally swells up. As the cells lose their water content the body slims. Its blood cells can contain 94 per cent water, but after hard labour or constant exposure to a hot sun this can drop to 40 per cent. If the level of water in a human's blood cells dropped to 80 per cent, he or she would be dead.

Camels have a keen sense of smell and can detect water several miles away. When my camel stretched out his neck in front of him and increased his pace I knew he had smelt water, a feat that saved my life in 2002 once during a three-and-a-half-month crossing of the Sahara desert with camels from Kukawa in Nigeria to Tripoli in Libya. In addition, when a camel exhales he does not lose much moisture. Warm moist air when breathed out is trapped in a camel's nasal membranes and the tiny blood cells in those membranes return this air to the bloodstream. As a camel's nose is 18° Celsius cooler than the rest of its body, the recycled air is cooler. How does its nose stay cool? By funnelling hot air through moist nasal passages.

The camel has muscles which can close its nostrils to prevent sand from entering its nose during a sand storm but which do not prevent the camel from breathing. It just breathes through a smaller outlet. A camel's eyelashes are positioned so they almost cover the entire eye to prevent the entry of sand. And if sand does get through this eyelash screen then an inner eyelid automatically slides across the eye's surface area to wipe the sand away. If this does not work, the camel can induce tears to flush out trapped grains of sand.

The front and back legs on one side of a camel go forward and push backwards in unison. This accounts for the totally different motion of a camel to a horse, whose legs move in opposition on the diagonal, the front leg on one side and the rear leg on the other side going forwards and kicking backwards at the same time.

It is not practical when riding, to allow a camel to walk for too long because the motion is rolling and unpleasant and you lurch from side to side which suggests a reason it has acquired its name, "the ship of the desert". Far better to keep up a jog trot in the manner of a horse's sitting trot. In this way you can cover the ground in comfort. You bump up and down if the pace of the trot increases, the bumps becoming bigger as the pace extends to a gallop. And when a gallop is reached a camel can outpace a horse.

When you have not ridden for some time you are a complete wreck at the end of the first day's journey: every bone seems to have been shaken loose; but very quickly the muscles adjust and the shaking positively renews youth and is a wonderful weight reducer. Like a horse, "the outside of a camel is the best thing for the inside of a man."

The feet of the camel are cloven with two boney toes covered in a webbing of tough leathery skin cushioned in fat. When the sole of the foot is placed in the ground it expands, making it ideal for walking on hot sand or a rough surface. The knees and underbelly are padded to ease pressure and to prevent injury when a camel lies down.

In recent years it has been discovered that camel milk is very good for people with type one diabetes. Not as a cure but as a means of taking insulin without resorting to a needle, as the milk has a very high insulin content and a very low fat content. We test-trialled a diabetic friend in Kenya who, by drinking three-and-a-half pints of camel milk a day, he managed to give up injecting himself with insulin.

The camel – what an amazing creature – the perfect animal for any desert – or for getting right around Lake Turkana.

# 2

# The Journey

*Go into the night humble like a child; leave your deeds and your pride by
the fire, for under the stars, you are less than sand.*
                                        Kanuri elder, Northern Nigeria

When Jasper drove me up on 1st March to Sandy Bay and the
Sirima Lugga from Ol Maisor, we arrived nine hours late.
We had not factored in the disruption a broken wheel rod would
cause. On arrival we found Josh and Ivan lying spread-eagled on
the ground, recovering from their great trek up the Suguta, and
a gathering of various friends and well-wishers who had come to
see us off. I set off on a short six-mile hike to get acclimatised to
walking in a temperature over 40° Celsius. Having been whisked
out of a dismal and cold English February to Lake Turkana via
Nairobi airport in two days I was badly in need of acclimatisation.

But the anticipation of setting out once again on a trek through
wild, remote country overwhelmed me. I have been trekking on
and off in West and East Africa and Central Asia for over 50 years
and I have never lost the thrill.

A long, tiring trek through bush or desert, whether on foot or
riding a horse or camel is not always interesting. There can be
monotony in following long sandy tracks, a kind of on-and-on-
forever feeling that saps the spirit as much as does the glaring
heat and dust. Camp life too has its disadvantages: sandy surfaces
harbouring ticks, jiggers (painful parasitical sand fleas), sand

flies and scorpions, filthy water, a lack of fresh food, spilt whisky, supplies ruined by rain, wet clothes and bedding, torrential downpours and hail, all these and more are dispiriting to even the keenest adventurer. Touch a tree and it is thorny; camp near water and you are eaten alive by mosquitoes; sit in the shade and you will sit on a thorn, if not something worse.

But for me, trekking through Africa and Central Asia was the soul of life and I could not get enough of it. Every new tract of country is an exploration, every new village an adventure.

As for discomforts, they vanish quickly enough. A long trek in furnace heat will always eventually come to an end. Drowned like a rat in an hour's heavy rainstorm you soon dry out before a roaring fire and laugh at earlier misery. For if you have the love of it, the joy of early mornings in rain-washed air, the evening cool when the ferocious sun has set, and all the incidents that the day has brought gives you a feeling of great satisfaction. And at night, bodily weary but surrounded by the sounds of the bush or the stillness of the desert and staring up at the brilliance of the stars above, you doze off totally at peace with the world. As for risk – without it, life is really not worth living.

Sir Richard Burton, Count Teleki's friend, the eminent Victorian explorer, linguist and searcher for the source of the Nile, succinctly expressed these feelings in a different way. Although we were separated in our travels by over a century, I fully subscribe to the following passage from his book, *A Pilgrimage to Meccah and Medina*, one of the greatest books of camel and desert travel ever written:

> There is a keen enjoyment in mere animal existence. The sharp appetite disposes of the most indigestible food; the sand is softer than a bed of down, and the purity of the air puts to flight a dire cohort of diseases. Hence it is that both sexes and every age, the most material as well as the most imaginative of minds, the tamest citizen, the parson, the old maid, the peaceful student, the spoilt child of civilisation, all feel their hearts dilate and their pulses beat strong as they look down from their dromedaries upon the glorious Desert. And believe me, when once your tastes

have conformed to the tranquillity of such travel, you will suffer real pain in returning to normal civilisation. You will anticipate the bustle and the confusion of artificial life, its luxury and its false pleasures with repugnance. Depressed in spirits, you will feel incapable of mental or bodily exertion. The air of cities will suffocate you, and the careworn and cadaverous countenances of its citizens will haunt you like a vision of judgement.

And that was written before the advent of the infernal combustion engine.

Our camels were grazing contentedly nearby. As browsing for the camels would be in short supply it was planned they should carry their own rations such as early weaning pellets or nuts, and were given boluses which contain all the necessary vitamins and minerals to give them extra muscle and a fitness boost for such an arduous undertaking. They were also dipped against ticks and flies. Only the fittest camels of prime age had been selected. They seemed to be in excellent condition and not to have suffered too much from their Suguta experience. At Ol Maisor they had been taught to cross rivers and to swim. And many a long discussion had taken place as to how to get from the eastern bank to the western bank of the Omo. One idea was that they should wear inflated inner tubes around their long necks to keep their heads above water. At the same time two empty 44-gallon drums were to be strapped on each side of the camels to keep them buoyant. Neither of these ideas had materialised because in Nairobi, Josh had met an extraordinary individual called Halewijn Scheurmann.

Halewijn had grown up in the Pyrenees; went to school in France; skied in Morocco at age 14; and worked for a Ph.D. in Political Science in Utrecht. He evolved from being a Dutch hippy in his youth during the flower-power period of the late nineteen-sixties, to the self-proclaimed King of the Omo in his middle age. He first visited Lake Turkana and the Omo River in 1993 when he fell in love with the area and focused on the traditions of the local tribes. His interest in anthropology later developed to one of full immersion in the tribes of the Omo River and the Delta. For example, he was initiated as a Hamar elder after competing in a Hamar tribal bull jumping ceremony. Since 2000 he had organised boat safaris through his company, Jade Sea Journeys, which had been established to take travellers to the northernmost part of the lake among the Dassanech and the other tribes in the Omo Delta.

Because of the drought and inter-tribal fighting his well-heeled tourists no longer materialised. But he knew the area and the people very well and when he met Josh in Nairobi and learnt of our plans he had told him he would attempt to ferry our camels one by one across the Omo, using his Ethiopian government motorised metal canoe. Josh had arranged for us to meet him before and after we had crossed into Ethiopia and elaborate schemes involving inner tubes and oil drums were thankfully abandoned. Incidentally, camels can swim – but only for a limited distance. They soon tire and would never have made it beyond a quarter of the width of the Omo.

2nd–6th March 2006

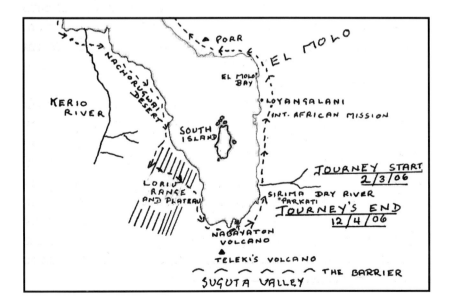

We set off at 6.30 a.m. heading for the town of Loiyangalani, the largest settlement on the lake.

I walked ahead of the camels with Josh and Ivan for two hours and then clambered on board and rode. I was conscious that I would only be able to complete this journey if I rode most of the way. We followed an unpaved motor road and I could see that on this relatively smooth surface the camels were moving well.

After an uneventful trek, we arrived at a mission station at 11.30 a.m. and were given a very friendly welcome by Barb Teasdale and Cheryl Hines – two American missionaries. The Evans family and the Teasdales had been firm friends for three generations. Their International African Inland Mission had an outpost near the lake and some years before the Teasdale family had treated Josh's sister when she was seriously ill with Madura foot (*mycetoma*). She was only one of very few people in the world to be fully cured of this serious fungal infection.

We had a very good lunch with Barb and Cheryl who were not at all buttoned up but fun and outspoken. During the meal Josh asked after their husbands. They said they were out searching for souls on their quad bikes. Jasper and I had indeed seen two quad bikes near South Horr on the journey up from Ol Maisor, being driven by two white men at high speed and with very serious intent. I was slightly taken aback when Barb said she was not happy with the way they were running around but I later learnt that they were heading for the headquarter town of Marsabit on urgent personal business.

During the lunch, and possibly because of the heat, lack of salt or having been shifted abruptly from chilly England to sunny Lake Turkana, my fingers on both hands kept curling into a ball and I had to prise them open to hold my knife and fork. I did not want to show my much younger travelling companions that the heat was having this effect and so kept talking while hiding my hands under the table in an almost vain attempt to prise my fingers open. I experienced great relief when we rose from the table and I could saunter nonchalantly away with my hands firmly in my pockets.

Before we left the Mission the two ladies prayed that God would walk ahead of us to keep us safe on our journey. In view of what happened subsequently, I am extremely thankful they did.

As we bedded down that night in the courtyard outside the mission house with the camels and the camel boys, there were loud bursts of singing, clapping and drumming which reached emotionally charged levels of excitement. The Turkana warriors were revving themselves up in no uncertain terms for a big fight with the Gabbra who, because of the recent drought, had invaded Turkana grazing territory at a place called Moite where the Turkana had established grazing rights. We all realised our route took us straight through the disputed territory and the fighting was likely to be extremely savage. Whatever, we were certainly not going to alter our plans.

Thankfully things quietened down about 1.00 a.m., but as soon as the drummers stopped, Barb's six guard dogs started to bark and then to howl. A howling bush dog kills sleep. Long gone were my Northern Nigeria days when, as a District Officer, I could call the local chief and instruct him to stop the dogs barking. As dog after dog in the town took up the chorus, we endured a miserable night and consequently were up at 4.00 a.m., sorting kit and loading camels, so we could leave at first light. This we did to great excitement from mission children of all ages who surrounded our camels asking countless questions. They must have numbered about sixteen.

Split between Kenya, Ethiopia and Somalia, the 500,000 strong Gabbra tribe, who were currently scrapping with the Turkana, might be numerous but their fascinating customs and religious beliefs are entirely unique.

They inhabit the Chalbi desert, between Lake Turkana and Moyale in Kenya, east and south-east of Turkana, extending into the eastern Chera plain, having fled the Ethiopian Emperor Menelik's armies in the late 1800s. Their name is supposed by some to relate to the Somali "Gabbr", an evergreen plant able to flourish in a desert environment. However, it is more likely to come from an Oromo (Ethiopian) word meaning "servant, or vassal" as they have adopted the Borana language, a sub-ethnic tribal branch of the Oromo people.

A nomadic people, their lives revolve around finding good grazing for their herds of camels and cattle, which combined, provide everything they need to survive in the striking semi-arid scrub land they inhabit. But while men dominate village life and are in charge of the herds, women play a vital role and are in sole charge of building Gabbra homes and performing the elaborate dances that signal the birth of a baby.

With so little water to be had, their beauty routine is an unusual one and involves anointing their locks with *ghee* (clarified butter) to keep hair smooth and shiny. Girls are given the most striking hairdos and wear the crown of their heads shaved until they marry, at which point the hair is allowed to grow back while the rest is plaited into elaborate designs.

But hair isn't the only part of life governed by the Gabbra's centuries-old laws. The majority of rules apply to children who, for instance, aren't allowed to call anyone older than themselves by their first name. Those names are also governed by tribal law and are inspired by the time of day they were born. Some are named after a major event, a ceremony, a rainy season or a dry season. Others are named after weekdays while a few get odd names such as ape, nose, tree stump and lanky long legs.

Whatever their parents decide to call them, all children are given a place in the social pecking order at birth – and once done, it is rare for it to be changed. The luckiest are the sons of village chiefs who are placed in the top grade at birth and show their status with long locks that make them resemble girls. As future chiefs themselves, no one is allowed to punish them, even when they misbehave, while their mothers gain an honoured place in society and are frequently asked to bless well-wishers.

These women are also given special jewellery to wear usually made from colourfully beaded leather, enlivened on occasion with Coca-Cola bottle tops. Those who aren't married to a chief, although often forced to share a husband, do get some special benefits including being in sole charge of who can and cannot enter their homes – spouses included.

Women are also in sole charge of raising their daughters and usually insist that they become excellent housewives. Men, when they come to choose a wife, will often judge the girl by her mother. The same principle is sometimes applied in our culture.

As we set out on our trek, here were the Gabbra, at the beginning of the twenty-first century, fighting the Turkana yet again. But in spite of the Turkana's reputation for toughness it must not be thought the Gabbra are soft. I once spotted a Gabbra filling his pipe with tobacco from a double-pocketed pouch. The two pockets lay side-by-side, one slightly larger than the other and joined together by a tough leathery sun-dried skin.

"What's that made from?" I enquired.

"It used to hold a Turkana man's balls," replied the Gabbra warrior with a slight smile. "I killed a man, cut this off, dried it, got rid of the contents and now have a much better use for it. I have also got a wife who is proud of me. Our women are much more attracted to a Gabbra who's got a pair of Turkana balls."

The journey to the village of Moite, the beginning of the "war" zone, took four days and on the second day we passed a sharply pointed, conical volcanic hill called Porr, which Josh, no stranger to some sections of the lake, had climbed six times. Dinosaur bones and gems had been found close by; there was a sand dune behind it and the western face was layered with sand which reminded me of the sand blasted against the sides of hillocks by the black sand storms in the Desert of Lop in the Gobi – called "black" because day turned into night at the height of their ferocity.

The travel routine, which we held to throughout the expedition, was to be woken between 3.00 to 4.00 a.m. by the admirable Josh with a steaming mug of well-sugared tea. I don't normally take sugar in tea but heartily welcomed the surge of early morning energy, which this sticky sweetener brought on. By 5.00 a.m., having loaded the camels and eaten a light breakfast, we were ready to set off. Even at this early hour the temperature was well into the lower forties Celsius. By 10.00 a.m. it was too hot to travel and we would pitch camp, occasionally striking camp and setting off again for another three or four hour trek at 4.00 p.m. Throughout the trip the average temperature hovered in the upper forties.

Answering nature's call in desert conditions is something I have done countless times since my Nigeria days. But squatting by moonlight at 3.00 a.m. becomes more difficult as one's annual clock ticks on. It's easy enough to sink on to one's hunkers in either youth or early dotage but getting up again is something else at 70 plus. Two years ago in Mongolia it became my daily agony when the temperature reached -32° Celsius and pee froze in seconds. Other people's offerings in the Mongolian squat had frozen, and such was the popularity of the site that great care was needed not to impale one's posterior on a sharp-pointed stalagmite.

Never one to waste a thing, Jasper had always been insistent that four sheets of lavatory paper was more than enough for any sized bottom of either gender, and he had drummed this mantra into me. But they must have been soft in the Navy (Jasper had been in the Navy during the Second World War). An ex-Army man, a little older than Jasper, told his daughter, Amanda, their ration was three pieces of Bronco, "one up, one down, one shine."

But in the dark, crouching in a sliver of moonlight with a howling Turkana wind and uncertain leverage in the calf muscles, even four was a meagre ration. Clutching exactly four sheets of Bronco, or its equivalent, and pulling up trousers was an exercise which sharpened the dullest early morning brain. If the howling wind blew the paper away, quick thinking was called for.

And sand can be rough.

In Northern Nigeria in the absence of loo paper, I found the air-mail edition of the *Daily Telegraph* extremely useful. It lasted for days and had the added advantage of providing out-of-date news while squatting on the *bayan gida* (Hausa for lavatory).

In one remote location, Tula in Tangale-Waja, Bauchi Province, I had a stock of these newspapers stacked on the mud floor beside the earth closet. As I picked up the top one, a spitting cobra *(Naja nigricollis)* reared up. Not only can they inject venom through a painful bite, they can also spit their toxins a distance of two or three yards. And they can move fast when they want to, and always aim their venom at the eyes with deadly accuracy. With pants down and eyes shut I shot off the privy moments before its poisonous venom, which can cause permanent blindness, could hit me.

The snake was later killed and eaten by my cook, Luttu.

My good chum Jock McClymont was always concerned about my long-term usage of newspaper – especially the *Daily Telegraph*. "You'll end up with printer's disease," he remarked drily.

Josh and Ivan walked all the way every day. I usually put in two hours walking but after that was more than relieved to climb aboard Makelele (the one who makes a lot of noise), my splendid riding camel. He had already proved his worth by extracting himself from quicksand on the second day, with my 13 stone on top. However, on the third day he was periodically snorting and vigorously shaking his head, an indication that he had the larva of a nasal fly or sweat bee up his nose. When the irritation became too great he would arch his long neck backwards and attempt to rub his nostrils on my thigh. At last, after a prolonged snort and determined headshake, he expelled a fleshy sweat bee larva, which landed on the top of his head and moments later after a determined wriggle fell to the ground. Once it hit the sand, it quickly wiggled out of sight. This larva had hatched from an egg laid in the poor camel's nostril by one of the numerous tiny flies, which hovered around his nose for most of the day.

These flies set up an intense irritation and the headshakes and eventual expulsion are all part of the fly's life cycle. Any attempt to deter the flies with spray or cream had little effect. They only disappeared when the temperature cooled.

Not so the camel tick, the commonest species being *Hyalomma truncatum*. These bury into the soft fleshy and vulnerable parts of a camel and were carried, come rain or shine, until the end of the road. All our camels acted as hosts to this particular species of *Hyalomma*. Attempting to pull the ticks out was greatly resented by the camels, due no doubt to the sensitive areas in which they buried their wicked little jaws. However, ticks can do more than cause mere irritation. It has been established that there is a loss of between one to three millilitres of blood for a tick that completes its life cycle on a camel and this can cause tick-anaemia and death. In some herds of camels in Kenya, tick-anaemia can cause up to a 20 per cent mortality rate in camel calves. A sufficient inducement for us to pull the ticks out with our fingers whenever we could.

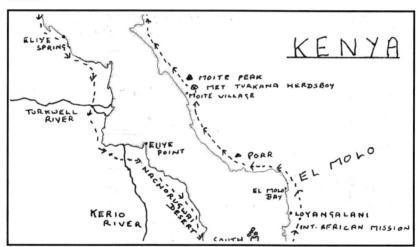

We trekked north along the lake's shoreline for two uneventful days until on 6th March at about midday we reached a solitary and prominent peak with a smaller, subsidiary peak called Moite (2726 feet), set amidst a craggy outcrop of rock. About 200 feet up, a sharp change in the colour of the rocks marked an old waterline, dating back a hundred thousand years or more, when the much larger lake was continuous with the Nile River system. That is how crocs and hippo came to be in a lake that is today widely separated from all other inland waters.

The lake reaches its narrowest point near Moite hill, which is directly opposite the Turkwell River Delta which lies twelve miles across the lake due west on the opposite side, where the river disgorges into the lake. It seems probable that one day, due to the massive restriction of water inflow to the River Omo that Lake Turkana could split into two at this point.

It was in this area, near the greater and lesser twin peaks of Moite, that Count Teleki lost four men in eleven days. He had shot a rhino not far from where we camped, and like us, he was travelling during a period of extreme drought. He commented in his book when their path turned eastwards away from the lake:

> Our men, no longer able to quench their thirst whenever they liked [*because they had left the lake*] seemed weaker than ever, and the effect of them on want of water was illustrated by the eagerness by which they fought for the loathsome, dull-green contents of the rhino's stomach.

There are no rhinos, buffaloes or elephants, of which Teleki shot six near Allia Bay and wounded several more, around Lake

Turkana any more. On their return to the coast Teleki's expedition came across a large herd of buffalo only about 200 paces in front of them.

> We waited until they were yet another fifty paces nearer and then ... fired shot after shot into the closely packed mass of bodies.

Even though they fired at least 24 rounds, they actually only killed one bull.

> On our way to him we had the opportunity of killing two rhinoceroses, so that our game bag today included five big animals. As this was more than enough, we gave up the dangerous task of following the other wounded buffaloes into the thicket.

These early expeditions of exploration involved over 150 carriers, recruited to head load the caravan's kit. These men had to be fed and the huge costs of these cumbersome and slow-moving expeditions were partly financed by the sale of ivory from the elephants they shot during their months in the bush.

The activities of "sportsmen" such as Teleki with their superior weaponry, were the start of the process of the rapid decline in wildlife all over Africa that has now reduced the vast majority of animal species to crisis levels. In 2019 it was estimated that 100 elephants are slaughtered every day in Africa, a truly horrific statistic. The human population explosion all over the continent, the desertification of lands to the south of the Sahara, the importation of workers and prisoners from China who have no concept of wildlife conservation and who will kill and eat any wild animal that moves, and conversely, the annual increase in sheep and goats – in effect man's profligacy and greed – have led to a situation in which it is hard to see if it can ever be redressed. The situation in Kenya alone is dire. Unless there is dramatic change, our grandchildren will only see the wonder of African wildlife in a zoo.

When I first went to Nigeria in the mid 1950s, Nigeria had a population of 44 million. In 1900 there were 16 million. Today there are almost 200 million. This leaves not only no room for wildlife – but little space for people. Kenya's population has increased from 2 million in 1900 to 54 million today. Uganda's from 1.6 million in 1900 to 42 million today. There was an increase of 7.2 million people in China in the year between 2019 and 2020. These figures are totally unsustainable and a similar pattern of huge increase applies in most other African and Asian countries. Rapid population growth is the root cause of most global problems; from water shortages to warfare and the catastrophic fall in wildlife numbers. The huge explosion of the world's population has greatly influenced man's contribution to climate change. We are a species which is completely out of control and yet those pontificating on political affairs rarely give population growth a mention. The elephant is firmly in the room but few people want to acknowledge it.

As we drew near the village of Moite, a mile or two from the hill, women and children scattered in all directions, thinking we might be part of a raiding or "official" party. Their cattle, sheep and goats, which they were herding south to avoid the battle zone, wandered off quite unperturbed into the surrounding bush.

Josh and Ivan went into Moite village to talk to the village elders in an attempt to try to find out what exactly was going on. They came back with inconclusive information, but they did learn that fighting usually takes place between 1.00 p.m. and 6.00 p.m. and a truce is called at nightfall so that both sides can eat and sleep.

No night operations for them.

We pitched camp about a mile from the village and about 3.00 p.m. a young Turkana herdsboy, no more than a ten-years-old, walked into our camp. He had an extraordinary tale to tell, as I wrote in my journal:

Apparently his immediate family had fled to Loiyangalani and had left him behind to mind their sheep and goats. He has no idea when they will collect him and has eaten no food for two days. We feed the poor frightened mite who begs me to take him with us. That we cannot do but we give him a further three days supply of food. He leaves us in the late afternoon but I have little doubt he will be back. He knows which side his bread is buttered and we are his only bread for miles around. And sure enough, an hour later, he returns pointing fearfully at a toothbrush shrub (*salvadora persica*) a few feet behind me. The branches of the toothbrush tree are a highly effective way of cleaning one's teeth and its berries are not unlike English blackcurrants in appearance and flavour, but with a tang of nasturtium.

"Keep well away from it," he exclaimed tugging on my right arm. "Two Turkana men were killed near the tree a week ago in the fighting and if you go near it," his eyes widened, "it will wrap its branches around you and squeeze you to death."

I thought how that would make a rather effective story, in a suitably modified form, for children who were reluctant to clean their teeth.

That evening two of the local home guard came into our camp. They did not say much but just sat and stared at us.

## 7th–11th March 2006

On the 7th of March we headed for Allia Bay, famous for its large population of crocs, which delighted in the shelter of this picturesque cove. The lake was the colour of jade of the highest quality, but these prosaic sights abruptly disappeared when we were forcibly reminded that we had entered a war zone. Moses discovered an unexploded Chinese mortar bomb and Kamau picked up an AK's magazine full of unexpended ammunition. We were clearly in the middle of an area where real action had just taken place.

We pitched camp near Jarigole Hill about eight miles south of Allia Bay under a solitary thorn tree, which topped a small rise, about 50 yards from the lake. The tree was called *Lototoropendet* meaning "the tree with the hole in it".

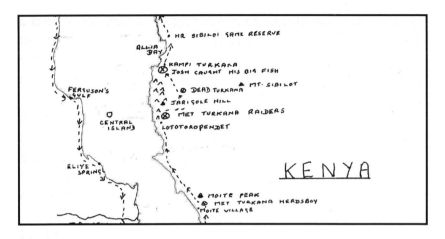

To the north of Jarigole (3,500 feet) a chain of hills runs out towards Allia Bay. Near Jarigole Hill is a famous archaeological site with mounds signifying cemeteries of an ancient people dating from *c.* 4,000 BC. In 1978, Dr. Frank Brown and Professor Craig Feibel of the Turkana Basin Institute and the Leakey Foundation's Scientific Committee discovered this Pillar Site, one of five known archaeological sites in the Turkana Basin that combine large, low mounds, pillars, platforms and cairns. In 1986 it was decided to excavate the site to determine if its primary function was that of a cemetery. Not only did this prove to be the case, but the material recovered from the first season of work, showed that the Jarigole Pillar Site provided the first definitive Nderit Ware, a most ancient pottery known to be associated with pastoralists in East Africa, who were among the first to herd cattle, sheep and goats.

At Jarigole, lesser hills drop sharply into the water in a series of rocks and cliffs, making a crossing with camels impossible. Josh advised that next day, we trek to the east for about a mile and then turn north along the eastern side of Jarigole and head for Allia Bay. I was looking at Jarigole through binoculars and was slowly lowering my field of vision, when I spotted six men carrying weapons, jogging along the shore of the bay towards us.

I immediately told Josh who suggested we should walk along the shore to meet them. I concurred. To allow them to come among us in our camp would be to invite trouble. It would send out a totally different message if we strode towards them and involved them in conversation. The chances were high they were Turkana and that they would be able to understand Swahili, which both Josh and Ivan spoke fluently.

Half-way round the bay where we had camped, the three of us stopped and allowed the warriors to lope up towards us, their AKs at the ready. When they stopped in front of us I noticed that all their safety catches were "off". They were Turkana, five in their early twenties and another man in his early forties – in African terms, an old man. The hair of the youths was matted, their eyes flashed from side to side and the yellowing of the whites of their eyes indicated that they were on drugs. They were also extremely nervous and one youth in particular kept stroking his AK's trigger.

They told Josh that they were the rear guard of a successful raiding party that had come across from the west side of the lake by boat to steal livestock from the Gabbra. The small stock had been ferried back across the lake in their boats and there were about 700 stolen camels heading round the lake via the Loriu Plateau. The seventh member of their party had been wounded so they had left him lying on the track which we would follow.

"You guys must be so hungry after such a successful day." Josh said to them in Swahili, "Come over and have some tea. If you give us that camel hump fat you're carrying we'll cook if for you."

This was a clever move. It showed we had no ill intent and were prepared to help. The youths looked at the older man who nodded and we backtracked and led them into our camp. Not unnaturally our own boys, two of whom were Turkana, were extremely nervous.

Soon the fighters had been very well fed, watered and given wads of chewing tobacco, which the Turkana love. The youngest youth kept rattling the bolt of his AK and staring at their leader. It wasn't too difficult to surmise what was going on in his mind. Then he asked the old man a straight question and the others stopped chattering and stared at him. After a moment of silence the old man shook his head. The youth was clearly disappointed and acquiesced. It wasn't until after they had left that Josh asked one of our Turkana boys what the old man had said.

"The young one asked him if they could shoot us and take our camels because the camels were very fit and healthy and worth good money. The old man replied that if we had been black men they could do that. But there are always more problems when you shoot a *mzungu* (white man). Better we leave them be."

After this the conversation lightened. They told us they had had enough fighting and were going back to their homes on the other side of the lake.

The old man turned to me and gripped my arm, which he stared at and then shook. "You are too old," he said. "When you get into Ethiopia the Dassenech will strip you of everything you possess and you'll return to Kenya stark naked." This caused much amusement all round. "That is if they don't kill you first," he added with a wry smile.

Their mood had lightened too, but they were still suspicious. Before they left us, the old man sent two of them off down the track along which we had come, to check whether we had set up an ambush of soldiers or policemen to catch them. They returned after about 30 minutes, gave him reassurances there was no one there and, with handshakes all round, they left carrying two of Josh's fishing lures which he had generously given them. After they had left we all went fishing, which seemed the most relaxing and therapeutic thing to do.

We only spent one night at Lototoropendet as the site was not a good one with little shade and next day, following Josh's plan to avoid the rocks, we left the shoreline and walked directly to the east. After about a mile we turned to the north and trekked through a sparsely wooded plain. As we crossed the furrowed course of a dry river called Nangurio, meaning the river of the giraffe, the ground was bare and only spasmodically relieved by clumps of dense growth which indicated an underground water supply. At midday we reached a sandy tributary of the

Moite River and stopped to rest. Debris stranded in the branches of acacia trees marked how high the river had risen before the drought.

Just after we moved off, our camel boy Barabara pointed out a concentration of vultures circling overhead about two miles in front of us. As we closed in on the object that was attracting them, we picked up the sweet, sticky stench of death, which completely overpowered us. The scrub opened up onto a parched clearing where the body of the dead Turkana raider, which the group of young warriors had told us about, lay on his back, bloated in the hot sun. His body had ballooned into a grotesque sight and I felt that at any moment it would burst. He had apparently been tortured and then killed when he was found dying of his wounds, and after 48 hours in the hot sun he was not a pretty sight.

We did not linger.

As we trekked on we came across more and more dead livestock, goats, sheep and camels. It was not pleasant to be travelling through a battle zone and a drought-stricken area and the stench of death was everywhere. We skirted up and over rough ground covered in rocks and boulders and after eleven miles arrived back beside the lake. Here we pitched camp at a place called Kampi Turkana and decided to have a couple of days rest. We were about fourteen miles from the Headquarters of the Kenya Wildlife Service Sibiloi Game Reserve and our camp was just inside the reserve. From Kampi Turkana we decided to push on towards the Ethiopian border. It seemed sensible to rest up before embarking on the long road ahead.

Josh was becoming desperate to fish. He had brought two rods and the right lures to catch Nile tilapia or the mighty Nile perch, but as a relatively novice fisherman he had, unlike his highly esteemed prowess as an experienced hunter, little piscatorial experience. I was as keen as he was to fish, but by the time I had hooked a cormorant, sitting on a rock drying his wings, and lost two of Josh's precious lures to overhanging rocks, my authority as a fisherman of even limited ability had utterly vanished and I was in everyone's mind, including my own, completely discredited.

I left Josh and Ivan making their near perfect casts into the lake and retreated in embarrassment. But embarrassment was abruptly banished when Josh let out a triumphant cry. His beginner's luck had been activated, he had hooked a huge Nile perch and for almost two hours he played it in a highly professional style until at long last the exhausted fish was hauled ashore. It was a whopper, almost four feet long and had sufficient meat on it to feed our whole team two or three times over. It must have weighed out at 80 pounds, a truly huge fish, but still a long way off from the 214 pounder caught by Edgar Barton Worthington (1905–2001) after whom two types of Nile perch were named following his pioneering researches related in *The Life of Lake Albert and Lake Kioga*, published in the journal of the Royal Geographical Society 1929.

As Josh held his fish up for a photo, grinning like a cat from Cheshire with its whiskers smeared with cream, Ivan and I proffered our congratulations. To catch a fish of this size from the shoreline was very unusual as the bigger fish tend to remain in the lake's deep water and not come so close to the shore.

Josh and Ivan spent the rest of the next two days fishing with Josh riding his luck in spectacular fashion and catching two more impressive Nile perch – some beginner! Having lost yet another of Josh's lures I decided to fashion my own from a trout fly weighted with an appropriately bent British Airways fork. Amazingly this worked and I caught my first fish – a Nile tilapia. Not quite big enough to eat but just large enough to restore some pride in my fishing ability, if not to Josh and Ivan then at least to myself.

At one point I left the two fanatical young fishermen and went on a solitary walk to scout out some nearby large ruddy-coloured boulders. This jaunt was enlivened by my encounter with a hostile troupe of baboons, scrambling about over the rocks. I have been wary of baboons ever since a friend of mine was dragged from his car by baboons on the road to Jos in Northern Nigeria. The baboons had put him into Jos hospital for over a week. I also remember when as a Mortar Officer with the Royal West African

Frontier Force my platoon fired their two-inch mortar and killed, quite unintentionally, three adult baboons. This distressed me at the time and led to my belief that one day baboons might seek revenge. Although almost fifty years had passed since that incident, who knows?

This extended family were barking angrily at me from all directions, having, no doubt, been stirred up by all the recent shooting in the area. I didn't bark back, I retreated.

Just before sunset on our second rest day, I decided to try to show the team how to make a table spin when it was placed upright on a metal basin, which was three-quarters full of water. This does not involve juju or chicanery. It is pure physics, a reaction of wood, metal and water when coupled to human energy. It is similar to a water diviner using a divining rod to find water – a combination of human energy, wood and water.

Professor Yuan Guoying, who successfully enabled me to enter the former Chinese nuclear test area to research the wild camel, had taught me how to do this and it had worked in such diverse countries as England, Mongolia, Spain and China. It had also worked in Nairobi and on Jasper's ranch at Ol Maisor. Would it work in the bandit-infested area to the east of Lake Turkana? That is what I intended to find out.

It is important that the metal bowl is not made of stainless steel, but is the kind of tin bowl that is used in most African kitchens and found in most African markets. The camel boys eyed me nervously as I partially filled the metal bowl with water and balanced our little wooden bush table upside down on its rim, leaving the table's four legs pointing upwards. Josh and Ivan whispered to each other and looked on with unsuppressed scepticism.

"I would like four of you to place the middle finger of your right hand lightly on top of an upturned table leg. Then," I continued using Professor Yuan Guoying's telling phrase, "I want you to empty your minds and stare at your fingernail. The table should then gradually start to revolve in a clockwise direction.

If that happens, then please walk with it but don't remove your finger. If it really works, the table will spin so rapidly that it will fall off the bowl. If that occurs you will see the water in the bowl spinning furiously."

The eyes of the Africans widened. Shaking his head from side to side, Barabara indicated that he would have nothing to do with such mumbo jumbo. They all thought I was dabbling in juju or the black arts. We started with Josh, Ivan and Lerebaiyan. They stared at their fingernails for fully five minutes and nothing happened.

"You have to think positive," I said. "If you think it's all rubbish, it will definitely not work." Ivan seemed the most sceptical and gave his place to Kamau. Once again, nothing happened.

I sensed that Epekor might be a better bet and decided to try it with just the two of us. I recalled how a large table had spun dramatically with just the Professor and myself emptying our minds. Epekor and I stood and stared at our fingernails.

Just as I was beginning to sense that the team must think I was completely off my mind, I felt the table wobble. It didn't start to revolve, it just wobbled. I could see that Epekor felt this wobble too. And then, first with a grating sound as it rubbed along the rim of the bowl and shortly afterwards noiselessly as, hovercraft-like, it rose up on a cushion of air, it started to revolve. All chatter stopped and the eyes of the spectators widened. On this occasion it did not spin violently, it just revolved slowly. But not for long, Epekor had had enough. He took his finger off the table leg and walked away. No African wanted it to go on. They had witnessed pure juju and nothing would persuade them otherwise. After this demonstration they treated me differently, not so much with an increased respect but with a certain wariness. After all, you never, ever, cross a witch doctor.

Before we reached the headquarters of the Sibiloi Game Reserve on 12th March we trekked across a large flood plain, which indicated the lake had been much wider in the past. We continued to see numerous carcasses of wildlife, which had died due to the drought, including a large herd of over 30 topi

*(Damaliscus lunatus jimela)*, the large antelope that is native to this area.

12th March 2006

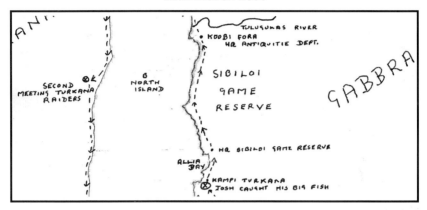

At about 8.00 a.m. we stopped outside the wooden hut, which served as the headquarters of the reserve. For a long time, tourists have ceased coming to Sibiloi on account of the inter-tribal warfare, drought and the Somali *shifta* or bandits, who periodically plague the area. The reserve was established in 1973 by the government of Kenya close to the volcanic Mt. Sibilot for the protection of wildlife and palaeontologist sites: it covers 610 square miles and in 1997 was listed as a UNESCO World Heritage Site.

Immediately on arrival, we encountered a typical African problem when the deputy director, a rotund and pompous man, denied us access to the reserve because he had not been informed that we were coming.

"I have the letter of authority from the Kenya Wildlife Service here," said Josh, waving the relevant piece of paper.

The deputy director studied it. "It was sent to the director and not copied to me. It also does not state the exact time of your arrival."

"How could we possibly have given you an arrival time? We've travelled through a battle zone with camels," Josh retorted.

The deputy director smiled. " I was not informed so you cannot proceed."

Josh reached for his mobile. "I am going to telephone Nairobi," he said.

12th March was a Sunday and the chances of finding the lady director of Kenya Wildlife Service Tourism at nine o'clock on a Sunday morning were pretty remote. But to our amazement she answered her mobile and smartly and forcibly instructed the obstructive official to let us through. His face showed his utter disgust at having to take orders from a woman.

Not to be defeated he said, "Yes, you can proceed but only if you take with you three armed guards to protect you from the tribal fighting."

"We have already been through the battle zone."

"How do you know they are not fighting in my reserve as well? If you get caught up in the fighting," his eyes widened, "maybe even killed, I will be held responsible. Each guard will cost you 1,000 shillings a day for four days," he paused to make a mental calculation, "That will be 12,000 shillings. I will give you a receipt and you can proceed."

Although Josh was angry, we all discussed the matter and decided to pay him.

Having settled the account, we continued over the flood plain littered with more dead and dying wildlife. I had seen people and domestic animals undergo extreme suffering in harsh climatic conditions but I had never before seen drought-stricken, skeletal zebra. It had always appeared plump and rotund in the driest landscape. To see them dead or dying and ribby, with misshapen flanks like a half-starved horse was a shock, and made me realise the dreadful severity of the current drought.

At about midday we reached a clump of shattered acacia trees, their lower branches stripped of any vestige of leaf, where we pitched camp. It soon became evident that countless sheep and goats all hosting two or three different species of ticks, had camped there before us. I rubbed kerosene all over my body in an attempt to make my skin unpalatable to the voracious "pepper" tick. It's a good "bush" tip that works if you don't mind smelling like a carelessly filled hurricane lamp.

Near here, three stray sheep had attached themselves to our caravan. There was so much domestic livestock wandering unattended in the bush due to the tribal fighting and the scattering of flocks. One of the sheep we named Fatima and Surbey, in particular, made a great fuss of her, fed her and let her ride on one of the camels.

### 13th March 2006

From my journal:

> Set off at 4.00 a.m. We pulled away from the sparse shade of the acacia trees and were soon back on the vast flood plain formed by the boundary of the old lake bed. This was ideal camel country and they travelled fast. I could only keep up by hanging onto a rope dangling by the side of the tail-end camel.

After two hours of being hauled along in this fashion, I accepted my limitations and clambered up on to the long-suffering Makelele. We travelled for a further 21 miles hugging the shoreline until we reached Koobi Fora, where Professor Louis Leakey's team had discovered one of the earliest humanoid skeletons in the late 1950s. The place now boasts a tiny settlement to house archaeological students, who come when tribal conflicts allow, and is managed by the Kenya Museum's Department of Antiquities.

On arrival we immediately became involved in another dispute. Having paid Kenya Wildlife Services for a four-night-stay in the Sibiloi reserve, the Antiquities Department, starved of visitors, wanted to charge us for a separate stay on their territory, which was of course still within the reserve.

"In which case we will leave at 6.00 p.m. tonight, trek for another three hours and then camp outside the reserve boundary," Josh said to the official who was demanding the double payment. "No stay, no pay."

Surprisingly the official caved in and we pitched camp in a rather desolate, treeless spot close to the shore of the lake. The heat was intense when later that afternoon we approached a tiny concrete, corrugated iron-roofed hut, which housed a complete replica of Lucy, *Australopithecus anamensis*, the female skeleton discovered on 24th November 1974 at Hadar in Ethiopia by Professor Donald Johanson, together with numerous bones and crude ancient implements.

Archaeological students come to learn and dig at Koobi Fora, but it is a very remote, hot and bleak place and most do not stay long. It was a two-hour walk each way from our campsite – I was utterly and completely whacked.

Louis Leakey's 1950s discoveries were only some of the earliest of several major archaeological finds at Lake Turkana. Formal excavations at the lake started in 1968 when his son, Richard Leakey of the Turkana Basin Institute, led a group to Koobi Fora, where aerial surveillance suggested that there were a number of human fossils to be found.

In 1972, Richard Leakey's team uncovered the skull and some limb bones of a 1.9 million-year-old *Homo rudolfensis*, known as "skull 1470" in the Koobi Fora area. The discovery reinforced an idea that was emerging at the time: that there was not a single line of early humans, but multiple lineages. It was already known that three other species were living in Africa around the same time: *Homo habilis, Homo erectus* and *Paranthropus boisei: Homo rudolfensis* added to this diversity.

In other words, humans used to be a diverse group of species. Later finds at Koobi Fora suggest that the three *Homo* species co-existed between 1.78 and 1.98 million years ago.

But it was not until the discovery of Turkana Boy, also known as Nariokotome Boy, that we began to learn about perhaps the most important of these species – *H. erectus* – who are thought to be our direct ancestors. They were the first hominins to migrate out of Africa, spreading into Europe and Asia. In some ways they were strikingly similar to us. They had significantly bigger brains than the slightly older *Homo habilis,* and were much taller. What's more, Turkana Boy revealed that his species walked more like us than older hominins did. He centred his weight over his pelvis as he walked, just like us. He also had arched feet and a relatively long stride. Turkana Boy was also able to carry things in his free hands while walking.

His family may have been carrying hunting tools, like spears. The anatomy of their hands strongly suggests they could do so. In contrast, our closest ape relatives have very little throwing power. These remote ancestors, who spent most of their time in trees, were probably similarly bad at throwing. This suggests that *Homo erectus* could hunt more intensively than older species, helping them to expand out of their territory. That would have been useful, because during Turkana Boy's time the climate was extremely variable. The forests his ancestors had thrived in began to change into more open grasslands, leaving early humans fewer places to hide from large predators.

In 1994, Richard Leakey's wife, Meave Leakey, co-ordinator of Plio-Pleistocene research at the Turkana Basin Institute made, together with her team, an extraordinary discovery on the west bank of Lake Turkana. They found another fossil like Lucy, *Australopithecus anamensis* (4.9 to 3.2 million years ago), which required moving the time line back when man first walked upright by about 3.5 to 4.2 million years.

A few years later, again on the west of the lake, her team discovered another species called *Kenyanthropus platyops*, or "flat-faced man". This species lived 3.5 million years ago alongside Lucy's ancestors. This discovery meant there were now several contenders for "the common ancestor" of *Homo*, and challenged the idea that humans evolved along a single line.

In the summer of 2015, researcher archaeologist Sonia Harmand of Stony Brook University in New York announced the discovery of the oldest known stone tools, dating to 3.3 million years ago. It had been assumed that only *Homo* species could make stone tools, but the tools were older than any known human fossils, suggesting that older species such as *A. afarensis* or *K. platyops* could also make stone tools."The tools are too old to have been made by the first fully-fledged humans." Harmand said in her talk, that "the most likely explanation was that the artefacts were made either by *Australopithecines,* similar to Lucy, or by *Kenyanthropus.* Either way, tool-making apparently began before the birth of our genus." Harmand and her colleagues proposed to call the new tools, the Lomekwian technology.

It is abundantly clear that Lake Turkana has played a pivotal role in our understanding of human evolution. We are lucky that this *Cradle of Mankind* was a geological trap, allowing us a glimpse into the lives of the earliest humans. But the current threats in the Omo Delta, which have shattered the stability of the lake, puts the future of mankind's cradle in great danger.

Josh had made an arrangement with Halewijn that he would travel across the lake in his hired metal canoe and on the night we were near Koobi Fora bring the much needed provisions for our camels, camel boys and us. I was looking forward to meeting the man who had been talked of in such reverential tones – the one man who Josh felt could ensure we crossed the Omo.

The light was fading as we settled down to eat the last of Josh's sun-dried Nile perch, when out of the gloom and the swirling mist rolling in from the lake, a tall stocky shoeless figure emerged, wearing shorts, a faded shirt and a broad-brimmed leather hat. He seemed to be in his mid-fifties, had gray hair and a look of absolute authority.

"Hello," he said in a guttural voice. "I am the King of the Omo."

A reputed character is not always larger than life on first acquaintance and an advance build up is not always realised, but there was an aura about Halewijn which made you sense that he had indeed lived a singular life. A man who would be king.

He chatted non-stop while tucking into our dried fish and washing it down with a flat, half-bottle of whisky produced from under his hat, then he stood up, belched and led us through the shallow lake water to his boat, anchored 50 yards off shore.

Fortunately, we could follow a ribbon of moonlight as we waded back and forth through the warm lake water. *"Brandy for the Parson, Baccy for the Clerk,"* or some such version of Kipling's poem, *A Smuggler's Song,* went through my head as I staggered into camp with yet another box of provisions. When the last load had been carried to our campsite, Halewijn, who had agreed to meet us when we reached the Omo River in Ethiopia, returned to his boat and disappeared into the mist.

14th–15th March 2006

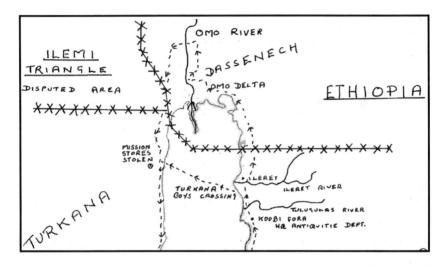

The next day was the day we finally left the Sibiloi Reserve. The rangers whom we had been forced to take with us from the reserve headquarters had long since fallen by the wayside. They were so out of condition they just could not keep up and they lasted no more than three days after which they slunk back to their headquarters.

Just before the end of the day's 26 kilometre trek, my camel's girth snapped. The camel saddle slipped to one side and I found myself dangling upside down on the left side of Makelele, my left foot firmly hooked in a stirrup. As my body thumped rhythmically against Makelele's side, he broke into a fast trot, my head inches from the ground. This admirable camel, who had looked after me so well, was the caravan's tail-ender and Josh, Ivan and the camel boys were a long way in front of me. No one was aware of my bizarre and somewhat hazardous situation.

Luckily, after five minutes of supreme discomfort my foot slipped out of the stirrup and I hit the deck. Although a caravan travels on average about two-and-a-half miles an hour, when you land dazed and dishevelled in a heap, covered in sand and dust, the caravan appears to move away from you with increasing speed.

Fortunately Moses, who habitually ran up and down the line of camels encouraging the slow-movers to stride out, spotted me, shouted to the other camel boys and the caravan slowed to a halt. He then ran back to help me and after a few minutes order was restored. I was back on board Makelele, and a new girth secured my saddle.

A disappearing caravan in a cloud of dust reminds me of the most wonderful camel I ever rode – Ahmed – a Bactrian, whilst on my last expedition in 2011 in China's Gobi desert. We were very near the escarpment, which forms the northern boundary of Tibet – the Arjin Shan or Altun Tagh Mountain Range. I was at the tail of the caravan, which was about 500 yards in front of me.

Suddenly I heard a slight noise beneath me and I realised I had dropped my whip. On hearing the sound, my camel abruptly stopped completely of his own accord and sat down; allowing me to walk back almost 30 yards to retrieve my chastiser. As I walked back to the sitting Ahmed my heart was in my mouth. I knew that if he leapt to his feet and trotted after the rest of the caravan I would be left far behind. To mount without help you have to lift your foot until it clears the rear hump of a Bactrian and then give a little spring jump, hoping you will land between the humps. If your camel decides to rise when your foot is clearing the hump the consequences can be both bizarre and painful as I learnt to my cost when my camel rose in that fashion from a rocky river bed. But Ahmed sat quite motionless allowing me to swing my leg and settle between his humps. Not until I gave him a command to get up did he stand up and resume his trot. A truly remarkable creature which had it been possible I would have dearly loved to have bought and kept.

Prior to my mishap on Makelele we had passed a herd of over

500 topi antelope and a ranger told us that 700 had died of anthrax the previous month. Both man and beast were undergoing a terrible beating from sickness and the drought. One interesting fact about the topi antelope, which resembles a hartebeest but is a darker reddish-brown, lacks sharply angled horns and disports a distinct hump at the base of its neck, is that it will sometimes lie down stretched out on its own, completely inert. An observer will think he has found a dead animal until, when only a few feet away, it will notice the intruder and will jump up and rush off.

We passed by a little bay, full of fat crocodiles basking in the sun by the lakeshore. They slithered into the water at our approach. We reached the end of this bay and immediately encountered a stretch of rugged black rocks, strung out over two miles. The camels struggled with the greatest difficulty as they crossed this unexpected barrier. We then crossed the almost dry Tulu-gulas River, which flows out of the lake, and yet another vast flood plain where there was not a scrap of suitable vegetation for the camels. Josh wanted to pitch camp but this was not possible without camel fodder.

It was growing dark when we finally moved out of the flood plain and into a thicket of trees and shrubs. An ideal campsite for man and beast. Just as we were unloading the camels a tiny dik-dik gazelle (*Madoqua*), which had been inadvertently separated from its mother, rushed frantically amongst us. Just as this occurred I noticed that the setting sun was in almost perfect juxtaposition to the rising moon on the opposite horizon. I had only ever seen this once before in the middle of the Sahara.

After breakfast on the following day, we divided up our loads to ensure we took only basic supplies for our journey across the Omo Delta. The crossing will be difficult enough for the camels without their being overburdened with non-essentials. Halewijn had agreed to take both this surplus kit, and our three Turkana boys who were terrified of entering Dassenech territory, over to the other side of the lake. We would pick up kit and camel boys after the Omo crossing had been completed and we had safely returned to Kenya. This load division obviously took time and having sweated profusely during the heat of the day, we were not finally ready to strike camp until 4.00 p.m. We then set off for the border town of Ileret, which we reached after three hours trekking.

Halewijn telephoned on his mobile to advise us to camp by the Ileret River just beyond Ileret township near the Ethiopian border, where he would meet us at sunset. We skirted around the township to avoid unwanted attention, and were immediately engulfed in a vast area of towering thorn bushes with wickedly sharp thorns. After an extremely uncomfortable hour in this hostile environment, during which we lost the track and our tempers, the thorn bushes abruptly opened up to reveal a dilapidated mission compound with a sagging corrugated iron roof housing American missionaries of a clearly fundamental persuasion.

In between bringing the word of the Lord to the Dassenech, the missionaries must have indulged in hectic coupling because the compound was overrun by countless semi-feral children of all ages. I had never encountered such strange people of the Book. As we walked past the gawping children and their parents, not a smile, a wave or a single friendly word was given or uttered. We were stared at in sullen and vaguely hostile silence.

I have visited countless mission stations all over Africa ranging from Roman Catholic smells and bells to Protestant happy-clappers. Whatever the denomination or schismatic divide, these missionary sects were, as their religion demands, invariably effuse in their welcome to a stranger. Here on the border of Ethiopia we were made to feel like heathen interlopers.

The river was not far from the mission station and an hour later we had pitched camp on a bone-dry riverbed. Shortly afterwards, Halewijn appeared, grumbled that we were not in the exact spot he had suggested, settled the details for the surplus kit and transfer of our Turkana staff to the other side of the lake, laid the plans for the visit to the Ethiopian post the next day and, in short, never stopped talking and scarcely paused for breath.

"We nickname him AK47 because he splatters his words all around him like Kalashnikov bullets," one of his staff told me later.

Supremely self-confident and opinionated, any opposition to his entrenched views were treated with utter disdain, yet Halewijn clearly had a very soft spot for the Dassenech and was held by them with a respect bordering on reverence.

"But they are changing every single day," he lamented, slapping his fleshy thigh. "In a short time their traditional way of life will have disappeared forever. Like Somalis, they are subdivided into numerous clans, which harbour age-old hostility to each other. During the times of year when farming does not compel them to stay on the land, they raid rival clans' farms, pinching livestock, women – in that order – and generally indulging in a silly season of inter-clan fighting. In the modern world its equivalent is a hard-fought game of inter-village football, except in the Dassenech's case, quite a number of the players never return home."

The fact that Halewijn had brought boatloads of tourists up Lake Turkana by water to see the Dassenechs' traditional way of life, had clearly contributed to their cultural collapse. He was helping to kill the goose, which laid his eggs of gold. The mobile phone, education and, as will be seen, the Chinese, have very sadly, finished off their way of life for good.

His other golden egg was his beautiful Kikuyu wife, Joyce Chianda, and he showed us a striking photo. But in this case poor Halewijn was the goose. He was killed while riding a motorbike on the Nairobi–Mombasa Road in December 2009, only a few years after he had helped our camels to cross the Omo.

Lake Turkana's principle source of water is the all-season, perennial Omo River, but its other two main water sources, the Turkwell and Kerio Rivers, are seasonal and only send water into the lake during the rains.

In the late nineteenth and early twentieth centuries, a number of European expeditions travelled to the region of Lake Turkana. Although diverse in intent, many of these were undertaken in the interests of furthering colonial territorial claims. Italian explorer Vittorio Bottego first reached the Omo River on 29th June 1896 during his second African expedition (1895–97), dying during this journey on 17th March 1897, aged only 36. The Omo River was renamed Omo-Bottego in his honour.

In 1900–01, Major Herbert Henry Austin led a British expedition down to the lake from Khartoum in the north. Of the 62 African, Arab, and European members of this expedition, only 18 (29 per cent) arrived at its final destination at Lake Baringo in Kenya. The expedition ran short of food supplies when it arrived at the northern end of Lake Turkana in April 1901. For the next four months the members of the expedition struggled down the west side of the lake and beyond. Major Austin himself suffered from severe scurvy with retinal haemorrhages, which left him partially blind in his right eye.

He found that an Ethiopian expedition, led by Ras Wolda Giyorgis, had, on the 7th April, planted Ethiopian flags on the northern shore of Lake Turkana, as well as having plundered the locals and reduced them to near-poverty. Soon afterwards a Russian officer Lieutenant Alexander Bulatovich, a confidant of King Menelek II, led a second Ethiopian expedition which reached the lake on 21st August 1899, and was equally destructive. Despite this, Frenchmen in the party accurately mapped for the first time many of the meanders of the Omo Delta. This map of the Omo River remained in use until the 1930s when Italian colonial cartographers made a new and more accurate chart of the river and its delta.

For the Omo's last few miles in Ethiopia (Abyssinia) it winds through low flatlands, sometimes overflowing its banks thus providing the surrounding countryside with rich alluvial soil and thereby creating large acres of prime agricultural land. In this isolated, lush and semi-tropical river delta, to the north of Gabbra tribal lands, lives the Dassanech tribe, a people who till the fertile soil, which is so rich it can provide them with two crops of guinea-corn and millet a year.

Dassanech traditions are clear on their point of origin. Everyone agrees they originated on the western side of the lake but were driven into their productive stronghold by the activities of the warlike Turkana tribe at the end of the eighteenth century. As the Dassanech retreated into their new territory, they quickly

overcame opposition from a number of small and scattered tribes
– pastoralists, hunters and fishermen – who lived in the area.
As a consequence of their migration, the Dassanech were saved
from the huge losses of cattle and human life, which the Gabbra
suffered at the end of the nineteenth century.

The Dassanech soon discovered that their fertile land stayed
productive even when their neighbours to the south were
suffering the effects of extreme drought. During the nineteenth
century rinderpest epidemic, the Dassanech suffered some losses
to their cattle, but the corn and beans from their carefully tended
farms were their salvation. This was a lifeline not available to the
pastoralists further south.

By forming an alliance with Abyssinia, and by accepting, albeit
reluctantly, Abyssinian dominance, the Dassanech acquired guns.
They quickly developed their newly found weaponry into a force
to be feared and gained an infamous reputation among the tribes
further south. They regularly joined forces with the Abyssinians
to raid other tribes and hunt elephants along the eastern side of
the lake, and took welcome revenge on their old enemies, the
Turkana, to the west. This uneven match was only squared when
the Turkana themselves acquired rifles. The Dassanech were
not a peace-loving tribe of farmers. They added raiding to their
capabilities and became a scourge to neighbours and wildlife
alike and a huge threat to law and order. They managed to
continue their needling raids for many decades after the advent
of Europeans.

Small wonder that when we were about to enter their territory,
our Turkana camel boys would not come. They knew if the
Dassanech found we were travelling with Turkanas they were
very likely to be killed.

16th–18th March

Our visit to the border post on 16th March was without incident.
Two long-faced and somewhat dour Ethiopians stamped our
passports for a three-day visa, and we were in and out of their

thatched mud hut in less than half an hour. And, most surprisingly, they had not even asked us for a "tip".

"I can fix these things," bragged Halewijn when we met up with him that evening. "Nothing is impossible for the King."

I noticed that near the immigration hut was a string of over 50 broken-down East European tractors. And a huge pile of twisting and rusted irrigation pipes. "The result of a failed North Korean agricultural project initiated under Menigistu," Halewijn explained, alluding to Ethiopia's brutal rebel and, from 1974, Marxist dictator – responsible for between one and two hundred thousand deaths – who is still alive, and has recently written his memoirs.

As he was speaking we heard a distant rumble although the sky was completely clear of clouds.

"Flash flood," muttered Halewijn. "Come on, run like hell or you will lose all your kit."

We scrambled back to the riverbed and saw that our camel boys were already piling our kit onto the bank of the river. Halewijn raced across the riverbed and climbed up the riverbank on the other side where he had left his jeep. Twenty minutes later it came, a roaring torrent of gurgling dark brown water. The sky above was still cloudless and blue – a flash flood can take place without warning even if you have seen no rainfall whatsoever.

Halewijn having picked up our surplus kit shortly after midnight, we advanced in bright moonlight into Ethiopia and Dassenech country. What a contrast to the drought-stricken lands further to the south. Here, growing in the fertile silt of the delta, were numerous healthy crops of guinea corn, maize and millet. So fertile is the flood-plain of the Omo Delta that farmers can harvest two crops a season. Men, women, children and livestock all looked sleek, fit and healthy, in stark contrast to the ravaged herds of wildlife, livestock and people we had encountered in Sibiloi. Not since my time in Northern Nigeria had I seen tiny children perched on makeshift platforms made from guinea corn stalks, rattling tins filled with pebbles to keep predatory birds at bay. We were emerging from a parched desert into a fertile oasis and it was little wonder that the Dassenech would not tolerate any alien tribesmen entering their precious territory. The condition of the people and their crops had certainly improved since the British explorer and hunter Arthur Neumann, of whom more later, arrived here in 1895.

He wrote that:

> The people of these districts live from hand to mouth beginning to eat the green Millett as soon as the grain is formed, so that, though they keep on planting crop after crop, as each is reaped, not only have they none to spare for sale but they are themselves often in straits for food.

This was certainly not the case at the time of our visit.

The Dassenech, some of whom were dressed in leather loincloths, sported picturesque coloured skullcaps and not since my days on the Cameroun border 40 years previously had I encountered adult women dressed in cow skins down to the ankles. This was certainly not camel country and the camels fascinated the Dassenech. But the Omo Delta is not a good place for camels, horses or donkeys. It is here that the deadly tsetse fly, harbinger of sleeping sickness and death, abounds.

The tsetse fly is a large biting fly that lives by feeding on the blood of vertebrate animals. They are long-lived and produce four broods a year and up to 31 broods over their lifespan. Tsetse can be distinguished from other large flies by two easily observed features. They fold their wings completely when they are resting so that one wing lies over their abdomens directly on top of the other. They also have a long proboscis, which extends directly forward and is attached by a bulb to the bottom of their heads.

Tsetse were absent from much of southern and eastern Africa until colonial times. The accidental introduction of rinderpest in 1887 killed most of the cattle in these parts of Africa and the resulting famine removed much of the human population. Thorny bush, ideal for the tsetse fly, grew where there had once been good grazing for the pastoralists and this land was quickly repopulated by wildlife. The tsetse fly soon colonised the whole region, effectively excluding the reintroduction of farming and animal husbandry. Some conservationists have described sleeping sickness as "the best game warden in Africa".

This depopulated and wild Africa was formed in the nineteenth century by disease – a combination of rinderpest and the tsetse fly. The rinderpest virus was accidentally imported in livestock brought by an Italian expeditionary force to Eritrea. It spread rapidly, reaching Ethiopia by 1888, the Atlantic coast by 1892 and South Africa by 1897. In addition, the white man brought with him influenza, smallpox and venereal diseases, all of which were killers.

Rinderpest, a cattle plague emanating from central Asia, inducing fever, diarrhoea, mucosa oral erosions, lymphoid necrosis and ultimately death, killed over 90 per cent of the cattle of the Maasai and other East African tribes. With no native immunity, most of the cattle population – some 5.5 million – died in southern Africa. Pastoralists were left with no animals, their source of food security and therefore survival, and farmers were deprived of their working animals for ploughing and irrigation. The pandemic coincided with a period of drought, causing widespread famine. It's estimated that two-thirds of the Maasai tribe died in 1891. Rinderpest ravaged Africa for over a century, and was only finally eradicated in 2001.

Wild mammal populations, with a natural immunity to tsetse, increased rapidly. The highland regions of East Africa, which had previously been free of tsetse, were colonised by the fly. And this brought sleeping sickness to the highlands, *Trypanosomiasis*, a nauseating, slow-working but invariably fatal infection of the blood, until then unknown in the area.

In the sultry, moist climate of the Omo Delta, tsetse flies flourished. Josh and Ivan were only too well aware of this and were anxious to take the camels across the Omo and out of Ethiopia as quickly as possible. They would only relax when we had left the delta and entered the tsetse-free environment, which surrounded the lake. Swahili, which the two of them spoke fluently, was not understood by the Dassenech, and this was another incentive for them to hurry back to Kenya as soon as we had crossed the Omo River.

Our trek through Dassenech territory continued some ten miles to the north of the lake and for the first part we crossed an area of relatively dense population. The bush, in part, was well trampled by the Dassenech's short, stocky cattle and in many of the denser vegetation patches; the triffid-like *Calotropis procera* grew, in abundance. It is a curious plant whose common name, Goat's Balls, describes its extraordinary fruit. It grows on hollow stems up to ten feet high like hogweed, and the stems collapse when you whack them with a stick. *Calotropis* produces little purple flowers that are pollinated by ants. The ripe fruit grows into large, green, hollow balloons about the size of pineapples and its seedpods are covered in white fibres which, when the fruit ripens, are borne away by the wind. Some tribes use the fibre for stuffing pillows and the tough stems make reasonable rope. Where cattle have degraded the land it thrives. *Calotropis* also has medical uses; for rheumatism, lumbago, sciatica, asthma, bronchitis, pneumonia, migraines, headaches, colds and coughs.

We trekked through a pasture of stunning little white flowers, favoured for their nectar by bees, and low trees in full leaf, full of twittering birds and heavy with the parasitic vine *Cissus quadrangularis*, a swaying evergreen crown of fleshy, quad-rangular branches, with ivy-shaped leaves and red berry fruits, sometimes popularly known as Devil's Backbone. This vine is commonly associated with species of acacia in dry bush country where it seldom produces leaves. Here in this fertile environ-ment and steamy humidity it flourishes. Where it has no trees to latch on to, it forms a mat, which hangs down over cliffs and rock faces sometimes with dramatic effect.

The Turkana use an infusion of the pounded stems in water to cure their calves of diarrhoea, although in humans it has been used, seemingly since antiquity, notably in India, for the treatment of asthma, haemorrhoids, wounds, fractured or broken bones, ligaments and tendons, boils, burns, as an analgesic for rheumatic pains, and indigestion. The fruits are also eaten and the seeds are used to produce cooking oil.

Termite mounds, a particularly favourite haunt of *Cissus quadrangularis*, appeared and became a regular feature of the meadowland through which we walked. Crested larks sometimes hovered tantalisingly close singing their shrill song and then swooping away behind the slender chimneys of mud thrown up by the activities of the termites, or white ants. The termite colonies live in barrel-shaped piles beneath tall ventilating chimneys where they tend their fungus gardens, look after their queen and store food brought in by fellow foragers from outside. The length and direction of the openings of the chimneys are designed to keep the temperature of the fungus garden at precisely 31° Celsius.

When we later crossed an area of damp soil, dark-banded, translucent-winged, black dragonflies rose up in clouds, some settling on the camels' backs and their loads. Sometimes their wings would beat so fast the black bands on their wings appeared to detach themselves from the dragonflies' body. After the harshness of the blighted and drought-stricken country further south we were trekking through a land of pure delight.

An ornithologist who visited the Omo Delta shortly after our expedition recorded:

> We had decided to leave predawn to avoid the intense midday heat. This wise choice provided us with excellent nocturnal sightings. These included Donaldson-Smith's Nightjar, Three-banded Courser, Black-faced and Lichtenstein's Sandgrouse, Senegal Galago (diminutive nocturnal primates), a family of Bat-eared Foxes, Black-backed Jackal, Common Genet and several other small mammalian fauna.
>
> As the sky turned rosy with dawn, we stopped for some excellent additions to our burgeoning bird list. These included busy flocks of bizarre Vulturine Guineafowl; Kori Bustard (reputably the world's heaviest flying bird), and its small relative, the Buff-crested Bustard; Black-headed Lapwing, Yellow-throated Spurfowl, Pink-breasted Lark, Red-fronted Warbler and both

Steel-blue and Straw-tailed Whydahs, common in sub-Saharan Africa.

A fruitful outing indeed.

By late afternoon, two hours before sunset, we had pitched camp near a bank of one of the delta's branches and Josh, Ivan and Halewijn's English-speaking guide, Lalle, lowered themselves into the water to see if it was a suitable place for camels to cross. Too much soft silt and too strong a current was the verdict.

Before this testing of the water, a watery test of a very different kind took place. Some of the Dassenach alleged that Turkana spies were lurking in our team and suspected that Ekapor and Lerebaiyan were the enemy in disguise. Lalle suggested there was only one sure way of finding out; the Turkana do not practice circumcision but the Dassenech who were Maa speakers are all cut, a telling difference between the tribal groups. The matter could easily be determined by a lowering of trousers. Agreement was reached and everyone, including Josh and Ivan, went down to the river to bathe while the Dassenech carried out an individual inspection. Satisfied with the outcome, the situation was defused, but no wonder our three Turkana boys had refused to enter Dassenech territory.

To save embarrassment all round, I was excluded from this anatomical inspection.

After a fitful night enlivened by numerous riverside bugs of every description, including scorpions, the testing of the strength of the underwater surface was conducted in a different place on the following day. After three attempts the team felt that they had found a possible route, which the camels would be able to reconnoitre.

Two strong camels, Sakafu, who weighed in at 1,873 pounds, and Naibor were selected as guinea pigs, but as soon as they entered the water they sank through the thin crust and into the silt. The experiment ended in complete disaster. The more they struggled the deeper they sank and no amount of heaving and pulling could extract them.

After three hours, the poor trussed-up camels were eventually extracted from the sludge and pulled to the top of the riverbank by up to a hundred Dassenech youths hauling on ropes. Obviously, the fee for the communal labour of one hundred Dassenechs stretched the expedition budget.

Much heated discussion ensued and finally Halewijn phoned in to say he had managed to hire a government boat with an outboard motor. If we travelled in a northerly direction where the delta merged into the Omo, he would attempt to take our camels across the river one by one, strapped to the side of this boat.

"That rain last night has increased the flow of the river," he said. "There is quite a current. It will be a tough job."

It rained hard that night and the noise of the river grew louder as the strength of the current increased. We sheltered under a hefty canvas draped over the camel boxes and were joined for the night by a million mosquitoes in search of their evening meal.

Sunday, 19th March 2006
The day we crossed the Omo River at 4.70N 36.06E

I think my journal entry best describes this momentous day:

> After walking seven miles in sultry heat through a long line of shady thorn trees, we pitch a temporary camp under an ancient fig tree to wait for Halewijn. He had arranged to meet us with the government metal-lined boat later that afternoon. It seemed an ideal spot, not far from the river and with abundant shade. Unfortunately, the gnarled roots of the fig tree hosted an army of scorpions who received their commander's marching orders once they spotted us recumbent on the ground. When we noticed them advancing towards us we leapt up and in no time I had killed five and the others many more.
>
> Shortly after this drama we were surrounded by inquisitive young Dassenech bloods who chortled and laughed while at the same time glancing acquisitively at our kit. Once again I noted how healthy and happy they seemed in their land of plenty. But

mission influences frequently came to the fore and I sensed they will soon be turned into people like Halewijn's boy Lalle, whose loud-mouthed and half-baked ideas were by this time beginning to irritate.

"What is the matter with you?" and "Who do you think you are?" were stock phrases he used to abuse his fellow tribesmen. These had no doubt been picked up from his master.

Halewijn, ever punctual and efficient, arrived with the government boat at the agreed hour. I was relieved to see it had a sturdy outboard engine. In spite of his self-importance, Halewijn is full of supremely practical ideas and in no time he had demonstrated that by hooking a rope under a camel's forelegs and by passing another rope under its belly it could, with the addition of a doubled rope harness, be controlled by a boatload of Dassenechs clinging on to the ropes and headgear.

The first camel bellowing and protesting was roped up in this way, manhandled down the steep river bank by almost twenty Dassenech ably assisted by Ivan, who when the camel was in the water, jumped into the boat and secured it to one side. When the first camel was under control there was a huge round of applause, Halewijn started the engine and the boat headed for the far shore which appeared to be almost the length of two football pitches away. Halewijn had to steer up stream against the fast-flowing current and then allow the boat to drift down to the chosen disembarkation point. As the river was a haven for crocodiles, a number of Dassenech, employed as stone throwers, lobbed rocks into the water at the first sign of croc activity.

After the first camel had safely been landed on the other side Halewijn returned to pick up the next camel which by that time was all roped up and ready to go. The whole operation went remarkably smoothly and it took just under three hours to land the 18 camels safely on the other side. A far shorter time than we had envisaged.

What intrigued me was that once half a dozen camels had successfully made the crossing and were silhouetted against the skyline, heads down and happily grazing, herd instinct took control. By the time the last few camels remained they were jumping into the water impatient to be roped up to join their teammates.

When all of us, our camels and our loads, had been finally

ferried across the Omo and not one camel, human or piece of kit had been hurt or damaged I felt a minor miracle had occurred. We had spent hours debating how we could make a crossing, from floating oil drums to inflated tyres we had explored countless potential solutions. When it came to the test, a boat, rope and Halewijn provided a solution which took under three hours.

Halewijn left us in a campsite surrounded by our camels grazing contentedly on lush foliage, completely oblivious of the fact they had made history.

While on the subject of crocodiles, it is worth recording that the Omo River crocs are thought to be leaner and meaner than their fatter brethren, which live further to the south by the lake.

Arthur H. Neumann (1850–1907), the British hunter and explorer mentioned earlier, was born on the 12th June 1850 in the tiny village of Hockliffe in Bedfordshire, the second son of the vicar, the Reverend J. S. Neumann. He spent almost three years in the 1890s exploring and hunting in the area between Mount Kenya and Lake Turkana. He wrote that, *"I hankered after the untouched wilds which I knew still existed in Equatorial Africa where the elephant yet roamed as in primeval times; where one would never see the wheel-marks of a Boer wagon* [He had fought as a lieutenant in the Boer War, taking part in the relief of Ladysmith, and before that in the 1879 Zulu War] *nor hear the report of any gun but one's own."*

Interestingly, he reached almost the exact spot where we made our Omo crossing and a terrifying event occurred:

On my arrival here . . . I had bathed in the [Omo] river standing up to my waist in the water which was deep close in to the bank, in spite of the crocodiles to be seen in the middle: for both I and the men had been in the constant habit of performing our ablutions in the lake where the reptiles were in plenty, and so had come almost to disregard them, though I never went out of my depth, or even far from the bank.

Late in the afternoon I went down for another bathe, with Shebane (my servant) as usual carrying my chair, towels etc., and did the same thing again. It is a large river and deep, with a

*Arthur H. Neumann*

smooth surface and rather sluggish current [and] deepens rapidly so that a step or two is sufficient to bring it up to one's middle, while the bottom is black, slimy mud. As we descended the bank towards the low muddy shore a native who was tending his crops said something to us, but knowing nothing of the language we could not understand him. Having bathed and dried myself, I was sitting on my chair, after pulling on my clothes by the water's edge, lacing up my boots. The sun was just about to set behind the high bank across the river, its level rays shining full upon us, rendering us conspicuous from the river, while preventing our seeing in that direction. Shebane had just gone a little way off along the brink and taken off his clothes to wash himself, a thing I had never known him to do before when with me: but my attention being taken up with what I was doing I took no notice of him. I was still looking down when I heard a cry of alarm and raising my head got a glimpse of the most ghastly sight I ever witnessed. There was the head of a huge crocodile out of the water, just swinging over towards the deep with my poor Swahili boy in his awful jaws, held across the middle of his body like a fish in the beak of a heron. He had ceased to cry out, and with a horrible wiggle, a swirl and a splash all disappeared. One could do nothing. Shebane was gone.

It was also near the shore of Lake Turkana that three weeks
after the terrible death of his faithful servant he had the narrowest
of his many narrow escapes:

> Advancing hastily thus, on the look-out for another shot, I came
> suddenly on two or three [elephants] round a corner of the path.
> Among them was a vicious cow, and she came for me at a rush. I
> say she, because, from her short stature and small tusks, I believe
> she must have been the same that had made the short charge
> earlier in the day. I could also see there was a large calf following
> her as she came, I stood to face her, and threw up my rifle to fire at
> her head as she came on, in a quick run, without raising her trunk
> or uttering a sound, realising in a moment that this was the only
> thing to do, so short was the distance separating us. The click of
> the striker was the only result of pulling the trigger. No cartridge
> had entered the barrel on my working the bolt after my last shot,
> though the empty case had flown out! In this desperate situation
> I saw at once that my case was well-nigh hopeless. The enraged
> elephant was by this time a few strides off me; the narrow path
> was walled in on either side with thick scrub. To turn and run
> down the path in an instinctive effort to escape was all I could do,
> the elephant overhauling me at every step. As I ran down those
> yards I made one spasmodic attempt to work the mechanism of
> the treacherous magazine, and, pointing the muzzle behind me
> without looking round, tried it again; but it was no go. She was
> now all but upon me. Dropping the gun, I sprang out of the path
> to the right and threw myself down among some brushwood in
> the vain hope that she might pass on. But she was too close; and,
> turning with me like a terrier after a rabbit, she was on the top
> of me as soon as I was down. In falling I had turned over on to
> my back, and lay with my feet towards the path, face upwards,
> my head being propped up by brushwood. Kneeling over me
> (but fortunately not touching me with her legs, which must, I
> suppose, have been on each side of mine), she made three distinct
> lunges at me, sending her left tusk through the biceps of my right
> arm and stabbing me between the right ribs on the same side.
> At the first butt some part of her head came in contact with my
> face, barking my nose and taking patches of skin off other spots,
> and I thought my head could be crushed, but it slipped and was
> not touched again. I was wondering at the time how she would

kill me; for of course I never thought anything but that the end of my hunting was come at last. What hurt me was the grinding my chest underwent. Whether she supposed she had killed me, or whether it was that she disliked the smell of my blood, or bethought her of her calf, I cannot tell; but she then left me and went her way.

My men, I need scarcely say, had run away from the first: they had already disappeared when I turned to run. Finding the elephant had left me, and feeling able to rise, I stood up and called, and my three gunbearers were soon beside me, I was covered with blood, my clothes were torn, and in addition to my wounds I was bruised all over; some of my minor injuries I did not notice till long afterwards, Squareface, on seeing the plight I was in began to cry; but Juma rated him for his weakness and he desisted. I made them lead me to a shady tree, under which I sat supported from behind with one of them sitting back to back with me; was stripped as to my upper parts, and my wounds bound up. I then told Juma to run back to camp as fast as he could for help to carry me in.

Three months after this narrow escape from death he started on his homeward journey. Weak though he was from his enforced convalescence, he managed to keep up with his ponderously laden donkeys and even managed to do a little elephant hunting.

It is interesting to record one of Neumann's tricks of survival *in extremis*. If suffering from thirst he would shoot a zebra, slit open its stomach and drink the stomach water. *"Clear fresh water,"* he wrote, *"would result from a correctly made incision; otherwise it looked like weak tea and had a vegetable flavour – after all its only grass."*

Neumann was described by one who met him, *as "a quiet, unassuming little man with a faraway and rather sad outlook on life. We had a long chat about game and the glories of the simple wild life in Africa. Neumann's native name is Bwana Nyama or the Lord of the Meat on account of his hunting ability."*

This quiet, unassuming loner, who during the course of his time in Africa slaughtered hundreds of elephants, had a completely different side to his character. In stark contrast to many of his contemporaries he had great sympathy for the African. Using the fewest possible number of porters and with sparse financial backing he managed to traverse some of the harshest country in the whole of East Africa, leaving in his wake befriended people from many tribal groups.

The solitary Neumann planned to return to Africa and held a meeting with James Sadler, the senior diplomat for East Africa at the Colonial Office in London with the intention of negotiating the grant of land and a government post in the Ewaso Nyiro River area of Kenya. This was agreed towards the end of May 1907, but the grant was never enacted as on the 29th May, after writing a brief note, Neumann, who was prone to depression, committed suicide with one of his hunting rifles at his lodgings in central London.

21st–26th March 2006

We had had to travel up river to reach Halewijn's boat and had therefore travelled beyond the spit, which divides the delta into two. There was, therefore, no further river crossing to be made. An early morning start saw us, at sunrise, trekking over a vast empty flood plain and we reached the Ethiopian border township of Namuruputh an hour later. It was here we would have our passports stamped to exit the country and return to Kenya. In contrast to our pleasant experience on entering Ethiopia, Namuruputh was a shambles. The surly and ill-disposed official did not even bother to look at our passports and wanted to refer us to his boss at Omerati – goodness knows how many miles away.

Eventually with patience and diplomacy he deigned to turn our passports' pages and then opined that the six miles no-man's land between the Ethiopian and the Kenyan border was a war zone inhabited by feuding Dassenechs and Turkana. He would provide us with a three-man police escort at a cost of 500 Ethiopian *Birr* ($60). Josh argued and haggled and eventually the sum was reduced to 400 *Birr* – but we were still compelled to pay them.

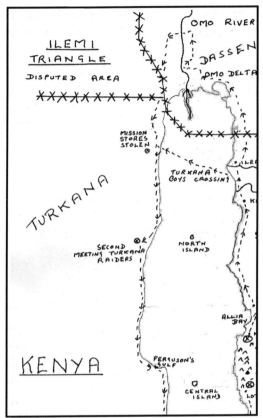

We said farewell to Halewijn's Lalle and set off with our escort towards the Kenyan border. Half-way across the sky darkened and we were drenched with torrential rain. Soaked but cheerful we were greeted warmly at the Kenyan Border post. I had enjoyed our time in Ethiopia but Josh and Ivan could not wait to return to their homeland.

We now had to rendezvous with our two team members, Moses and Surbey (plus Fatima) who had not wanted to encounter the Dassenech and who had sailed across the lake. This was not so easy as it sounded and we had covered 34 miles before we eventually linked up with both them and our surplus kit.

The following day was a day of rest and Josh and Ivan ventured off with six camels to collect fresh supplies which had been deposited in a nearby deserted missionary compound in preparation for our trip. They returned in low spirits some two hours later explaining that a large quantity of camel food, tinned food and fruit has been stolen. Ivan was particularly upset when he discovered the thieves had taken two precious cases of Ribena. I was more concerned about the missing whisky. There was not much laughter that night.

Over the next few days progress was rapid. There were long stretches of sandy shore along the western side of the lake, and the camels strode forward at a pace well in excess of two-and-a-half miles an hour. Josh and Ivan strode out and one day they covered 31 miles with me chuntering along behind them on top of Makelele. During this particularly long trek Josh had wired himself up with a gadget in his ear to teach himself Spanish. As he swung along in fine style, I could hear him muttering phrases such as *"Yo estoy muy bien gracias. Donde esta el lavabo?"* Josh's hunting career at that time involved taking Mexican hunters into remote bush areas in Tanzania. Clearly there had been a communication problem, which he was determined to resolve.

Our next big test was the Loriu Plateau, 40 miles long and 5 miles wide, and rising at its highest point to 4,800 feet, which was covered in lava. But for the moment, all that lay in the future, and swinging along at a good pace raised our spirits after the minor disaster of our looted supplies.

It was at times excessively hot with the temperature well up into the high forties Celsius. Josh had brought a large, black, shade net, normally used for shading vegetables. This was extremely valuable when we were obliged to camp in areas where there was no cover. Strung up with poles it provided shade of sorts in the oppressive heat and we would have been sorely tested without it.

Ivan, in particular, was assiduous in looking after the camels' health on a daily basis. They were by this time looking tired and had obviously lost weight. As browsing for the camels was in short supply it had been planned they should carry their own rations, such as early weaning pellets or nuts, and take boluses containing vitamins and minerals (cobalt, selenium and copper) to give them extra muscle and a fitness boost for such an arduous undertaking. They were also treated regularly against ticks and flies.

Nevertheless, when one morning my camel, Makelele, blundered about at 3.00 a.m., shortly after we had set off, it was clear that he could not see. Josh felt he must have been bitten by a tsetse fly but whatever the exact prognosis the poor camel could obviously not be ridden. Two other camels, Fujo and Charles, also suffered from partial blindness some days later, but with care and attention, extra mineral supplements and injections of Catosal, which boosts the digestive system, this terrible affliction gradually wore off. We were never able to establish the exact cause and whether it was a lack of vitamin A or *Trypanosomiasis*. Fujo and Makelele never completely recovered their sight, but Charles did and lived to walk many more miles on long safaris.

By this time, the other two stray sheep that we had acquired while passing through the Sibiloi Game Reserve had not survived, but Fatima was still with us and had grown very attached to Surbey who was absolutely determined to make sure she would survive until the caravan reached Jasper's ranch of Ol Maisor – which she eventually did. Fatima had become our lucky mascot and was being fed on very expensive multi-vitamin pills and our precious camel pellets to ensure that she survived.

Something very interesting occurred two days before our arrival at Ferguson's Gulf, a landmark site on the west bank of the lake. We were camped near some doum palms (*Hyphaene thebaica*) almost parallel with Turkana's North Island, when in the heat of the day two smartly dressed Turkana swaggered into our camp. One of them, an older man, ran up to me and gave me a huge, sweaty bear hug.

"You made it," he exclaimed. "They did not shoot you. They did not eat you. They did not take all your belongings. You are back home in Kenya. Congratulations."

I looked blankly at the man and then suddenly realised these two men were part of the gang we encountered on the other side of the lake, the Turkana warriors who had been on a killing spree against the Gabbra. Indeed, this older man engaging me in a stifling hug was the same man who had advised his younger hothead not to shoot us and take our camels, because dead white men would cause them too much hassle from the authorities. For a moment I was lost for words. Where else could this happen but in Africa? A man who was about to shoot you and then warns you that you will never survive the journey through another country, eventually meets up with you again, embraces you and fervently welcomes you back home. Only in Africa . . .

## 27th March–6th April 2006

On 27th March we crossed the Ferguson Gulf mudflats. Nobody seems to know much about Ferguson or what he did to leave his name to posterity. It is a barren spot in a wasteland of sand that is whirled every morning into dust storms by a gusting dry and hot east wind. Nothing much grows there except wind-blasted doum palms, scrubby bushes and needle-sharp grass.

We spotted a small fleet of abandoned fishing boats which Halewijn later explained to us in great detail had been part of a very expensive Norwegian Aid fishing project. According to Halewijn a Norwegian research team "discovered" that the Turkana are primarily a cattle people and the periodic droughts mean that every few years their livestock are devastated. This leads to inter-tribal cattle rustling and fighting over grazing rights, a situation which we had recently witnessed. What the Turkana needed, concluded the Norwegians, was a fishery, which would not be affected by drought, and which would stabilise the cattle owners' vulnerable situation.

The Norwegians therefore financed a $2 million frozen fish storage plant, constructed near Ferguson's Gulf, and built a $20 million road that connected this plant to a main highway, which linked the plant to the regional capital at Lodwar. The new Turkana Fisherman's Cooperative Society would sell vast quantities of frozen Nile perch and other fish species, such as Nile tilapia, to the towns and cities to the south.

However, when the power supply was switched on it failed after only a few days of operation. The amount of electricity needed to power the storage plant was far in excess of what the region could provide. The frozen fish very quickly became dried fish and shortly afterward evolved into totally unsaleable stink fish.

Then part of the lake vanished, the part where 80 per cent of the fish were caught. The Norwegians with their experience of Scandinavian lakes thought a lake was a lake and stayed as such for millions of years. But not capricious Lake Turkana, which fluctuates hugely every few decades whenever the Omo River ran low because of the periodic droughts which affect the region and result in famine – the very thing which the project had been set up to combat.

Norwegian Aid officials had already herded 20,000 Turkana to the lakeshore where they had been given nets, boats and sophisticated fishing lessons. When the project collapsed this population was left destitute. Many of the cattle they had brought with them had died from overcrowding and disease along the inhospitable lake shoreline.

As a symbolic white elephant, the Norwegian research vessel *Iji* was one of the boats whose rusting, rotting hulk we could still see. According to the official report on the collapse of the project "it appears to be damaged beyond the possibility of repair."

We reached a campsite owned by Halewijn where he charged his clients $1,000 a night to stay. That evening the great man himself returned with news and supplies from Nairobi. He had driven 350 miles in four days, mostly over unpaved roads, to honour his commitment to meet us at his camp.

During our chat that evening he told us that he had once been an honorary game warden in the lake area. The crocodile and turtle populations are much reduced, he said. The turtles because the Turkana eat their eggs in their constant search for food. On Central Island there used to be a huge population of crocodiles and it was a prodigious breeding ground. Today there were only 20–30 crocs left. Indeed, all wildlife species are in steep decline, according to Halewijn, due to the changing climate and the increasing demand for food as the human population numbers increase.

As if to confirm these gloomy predictions, later that evening one of the boats donated by missionaries, and now converted into a vessel of war by the Turkana, sailed into Ferguson's gulf laden with booty – Gabbra goats and sheep.

"I admire pastoralists," Halewijn said, "especially the Turkana. They harness nature and survive at the expense of other species. Long-term it's bad that our children will not experience all of

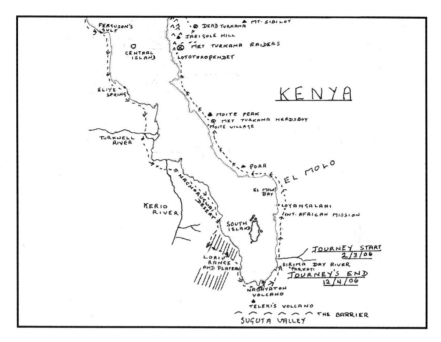

today's species. But do we have the right to stop species depletion or stop ourselves from surviving? Is there a religious obligation that we must survive as a species? That's the most important question I ask myself.

I believe when you see the carbon footprint of an average Turkana and compare it with the carbon footprint of any Westerner there's no comparison. There's at least a thousand-fold difference between Turkanas and Americans. Three Americans or five Europeans have a bigger carbon footprint than 600 Turkana."

The next day we passed Eliye Springs where there was a former upmarket but now abandoned fishing lodge. Halewijn said he would be giving up his tourist operation in two years time. However, it never happened. The lake and its people were changing, but I had little idea of the dramatic changes that would take place in a few short years' time.

The Turkwell River, which flows into Lake Turkana from the west, was almost dry when we reached it on 30th March and the camels had no difficulty in crossing. We camped in a delightfully shady spot near the point where the river enters the lake and soon attracted the attention of a number of friendly Turkana who, when not bent on shooting at the Gabbra, could be remarkably affable. Not being a good boy scout – I had absconded from a collective pack as a wolf cub – I had never lit a fire by rubbing together two dry sticks. Two Turkana youths taught me how to do it using two sticks and a little cotton soaked in kerosene. I bought an extremely sharp wrist knife from an old man and whiled away one or two hours in their company.

At one point an elderly Turkana strolled over with his gun, an old weapon not unlike a .303 rifle of British army fame. He proudly let me examine it and when I opened the breech I doubted it could be fired, as it was full of dirt and had not been cleaned for months, if ever. The parts were dry and worn with age and the round-nosed bullets lay tarnished in a leather pouch. He said it worked and had killed three men. I asked him to prove it by firing a round, but he declined, not unreasonably, as he said the bullets were too difficult to get hold of to waste on a dud shot.

Later we learnt that the 700 camels that had been captured from the Gabbra on the other side of the lake were camped nearby. I was supremely thankful that our camels were not among them. This thought was brought home when two more of the gang who had very nearly killed us turned up with their congratulations at our safe arrival in Kenya. Like the older man we had met earlier, they were very well dressed. Shooting up the Gabbra and livestock rustling was obviously a profitable, if somewhat dangerous, business.

On Jasper's ranch livestock were frequently stolen and if the direction the robbers had taken was not known he would send for Mama Muganga, who was a seer. On arrival, this old woman would squat beside Jasper, shut her eyes and after a few moments in a trance-like state would make a proclamation.

"They are just leaving the ranch with 12 of your cattle," she would say (or something similar). "Don't delay, get in your

Landover and drive quickly to the north-east. You might catch them in time."

It was important not to waste time because they might have a lorry waiting to be loaded with the stolen livestock, which would then be driven at speed down to Nairobi's meat market where they would become untraceable.

One day she was squatting beside Jasper as he sat outside talking to an old friend of his who had just arrived from Scotland. Mama Muganga abruptly looked up at Jasper and said, "Who is that man, is he a friend of yours?"

"He's an old friend, I haven't seen him for a long time."

Mama Muganga spat on the ground. "Tell him to be kind to his wife," she said.

This extraordinary unsolicited remark was absolutely correct. Apparently the man had just had a violent argument with his wife in Scotland and they were currently not on speaking terms.

I wondered whether the Gabbra had their own Mama Muganga who could trace their missing camels. I suspected they would have their own seer, because to the nomadic people in the area, cattle raiding and the associated killings are just another of life's many hazards or benefits, depending which side you are on. One only has to read accounts of the turbulence in the Scottish Highlands in the seventeenth century, to realise that livestock rustling and the associated killings are not confined to Africa.

One of the detrimental changes to this way of life is that the nature of raiding has changed. No longer do the livestock, that have adapted over millennia to their harsh environment, just change hands, but now get stolen at gun point and put on a lorry where they are driven to the nearest meat market for slaughter. The gene pool of these highly adaptable animals is being reduced to extinction, and their tribal owners are facing extinction as well.

The Lake Turkana area also suffered from the predations of the Ethiopians who periodically descended on the tribes in the Omo basin, to which they gave the all-embracing term of Shangala. This raiding became accentuated under the Ethiopian Emperor Menelik who died in 1913. As late as 1962 raiders were still descending from their mountain fastness in the Ethiopian highlands to raid in the delta, and in the Northern Frontier District of Kenya – the NFD – as it used to be called.

The British, during the colonial era, were never completely able to control the warring tribes in the NFD, especially the Turkana, the toughest of the tough. The vast area inhabited by the culturally homogenous peoples in today's Somalia, which had been carved up by colonial powers (including Ethiopia), and was later subjected to political interference from the Soviets, experienced extreme bouts of lawlessness.

In Somalia's case it is evident to this day in the form of the Al Shabaab Islamic extremists, and the Kenyan government, in spite of extensive infrastructure development, finds it difficult to exert authority over people influenced by religious extremism, and to whom warfare and raiding are a way of life.

The rains were building up and on two occasions it had rained heavily and we had had to scurry about with our big heavy canvas and haul it over the stacked wooden camel boxes, which Josh had methodically lined up to support the tarpaulin in case we needed shelter. After the rain stopped it became sultry and humid and the insect world launched an abrupt attack under our makeshift quarters with battalions of bloodthirsty mosquitoes forming formidable advance columns.

We were heading for the Kerio River, the last of the three major rivers, which water Lake Turkana. When we entered a little village, where we drank sweet tea and chewed on *mandazis* [Swahili doughnuts], youths, old men and mad women surrounded us with dire predictions.

"You will never get through the thick thorn bush which surrounds the Kerio."

"The rains have come. It's full of water, your camels will never be able to cross the river."

Josh and Ivan shrugged off these pessimistic forebodings. Our

# The Team

Lerebaiyan

Surbey

Epekor

Barabara

Moses

Kamau

Josh Perrett

Ivan Jensen

The start of the Journey

En route to Moite

Passing Moite Peak

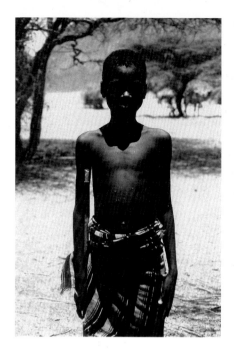

The abandoned
herdsboy at Moite

Turkana woman

Trekking on

Camel
killed by the
Turkana for
the fat in its
hump

Josh's beginner's luck

Chinese mortar bomb used in
the inter-tribal fighting

At Sibiloi Game Reserve

Killed by
drought

Lucy at Koobi Fora

Dassenech tribesman

The Omo Delta

Looking for a route to cross the Omo River

Our camel gets stuck

Crossing the Omo River

Crossing the Omo River

Crossing the Ethopian–Kenyan border

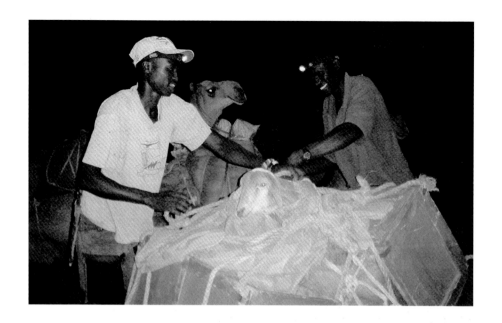

Fatima gets special treatment

Our camp in the foothills of the Loriu Plateau

Crossing the Loriu Plateau

Lava from Teleki's volcano

Crossing the treacherous lava from Teliki's volcano

The Team

Gibe-III-Hydroelectric Dam project

Lake Turkana wind power project

Gibe-III-Hydroelectric Dam project

Lake Turkana wind power project

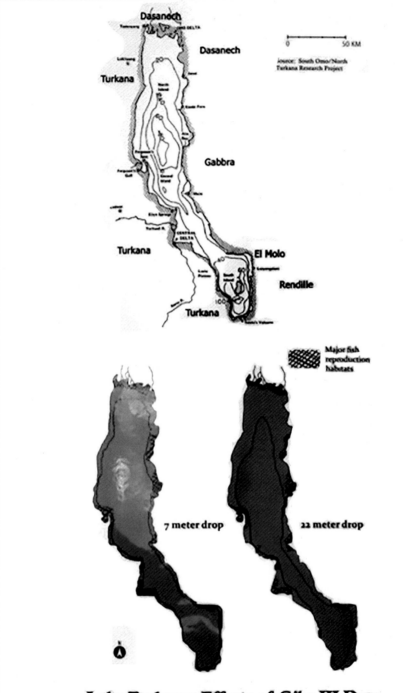

Major fish reproduction habitats

7 meter drop

22 meter drop

# Lake Turkana: Effects of Gibe III Dam
## (Bathymetric Map)

route lay ahead of us and forward we must go. As we neared the river we indeed came to a great thicket of thorn but with judicious *panga* slashing a way was carved through. And when we reached the river it was completely dry.

Ahead of us lay the lava-strewn Loriu Plateau and not one of us knew the exact route. A further concern was the possibility of encountering *Ngoroko*, a Turkana word meaning "outlaw" but which in reality encompasses, outcasts, murderers and bandits. Because of its remoteness and its inaccessibility, the Loriu had a reputation for harbouring such individuals. The plateau and the surrounding hills were situated on borderland between Samburu, Pokot and Turkana tribal areas but the "renegades" only came from the Turkana. Nearly every Turkana family had at least one son who was a *Ngoroko*, largely due to long-term on-going droughts in Turkana that created indescribable poverty and hardship. There were plenty of hiding places in the rocks and gullies and because of the lava there was no grazing for livestock.

Consequently very few people went there. We camped by the Kerio and it proved to be dire. Thorny acacia bushes, which made for hard lying, surrounded us and there was little grazing for the camels. I noticed and recorded in my journal just how tired they all looked. In addition, a strong wind blew sand constantly from the Nachorugwai desert on the other side of the river.

That evening, the setting sun sank steadily into a mass of jet-black clouds, which had puffed out directly behind the outline of the Loriu Plateau. Just as the sun was on the point of slipping away, there was an intense flash, which vividly accentuated all other surrounding colours. Blades of grass instantly transformed to a vibrant green. Dry acacia bushes shed their drabness and positively glowed in the extraordinary light. Even the very earth itself seemed to shine. I raised my eyes to the dark mass of clouds, which were tinged with the sun's blood-red glow, a sheen which changed every few seconds, starkly intensifying the jet blackness of the storm clouds. It was exhilarating, yet slightly unnerving. The overall effect lasted for only a few seconds. When the sun finally sank below the horizon, the whole landscape reverted to a dreary and uniform dark grey. I had noticed this phenomenon on one or two previous occasions in Northern Nigeria, but never so markedly as on this occasion. I am told that it also occurs at sea.

All Fools' Day and no early morning moonlight. As my poor, partially blinded camel would not travel in the dark, we had to wait until sunrise before setting off. After crossing the dry Kerio River we were confronted with the arid Nachorugwai desert. This strange desert landscape is divided into three distinct and separate sections; the first consisting of dead and dying shrubs and trees, the second a section of healthy vegetation and finally a series of dunes.

The crossing of this desert took about six hours and once we had left the last of the sand dunes behind we were ready to pitch camp. Unfortunately, apart from the fan-shaped spiky leaves of the doum palm, there was no other camel fodder available. Josh felt that the camels would not eat the whole spiked leaf, so the camel boys spent a further two hours gathering palm leaves and chopping them into small pieces. However, when the camels were released to gorge on this carefully prepared feast, they completely ignored it, went straight to the palm trees, craned upwards and tore whole leaves off the trees – which they then ate.

Leaving the camels to chomp away, we went to the lake for a swim. After a short time a strong wind got up and within two minutes had changed direction three times. I could see why the Norwegians had given up on their fishing project. Lake Turkana's unpredictable moods, like those of our camels, cannot be forecast in advance.

The next three days were spent trying to find the best route to follow over the plateau. The Loriu was not large in area, just a sizeable chunk of rock. But the whole of the plateau, the approach, the top and the descent was covered in lava. Lava comes in different forms. It can be a smooth surface of hard rock. It can be a mass of sharp jagged rocks which looks like frozen waves on a choppy sea or it can be wafer thin and brittle: the worst kind of lava of all. We encountered all three and the poor camels' feet were not designed to cross any of them. A camel's underfoot

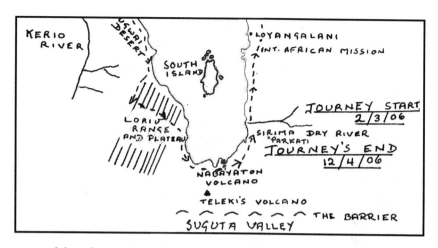

or pad has been described as resembling a tyre but filled with fat instead of air, it is soft and spongy and ideal for soft, hard, dry or wet sand. It is basically a cushion of fatty pads, separated by cartilage and enclosed in a fibrous rubbery sheath. Nothing discomforts a working camel more than having to cross sharp, insecure and sometimes brittle lava or rocks. Cuts and bruises to the pad are inevitable and puncture wounds are unavoidable. In Mongolia, after trussing up the invalid camel with rope so he can neither kick nor bite, puncture wounds and cuts to the pad are sealed with hot mutton fat, which, when cool, dries hard and acts as an antiseptic. I have also seen rubber pads, designed to mend a punctured bicycle inner tube, glued on to a wound.

We had no such kit.

A guide we had recruited to lead us up and over the plateau clearly had second thoughts and had scarpered. We were on our own and Josh decided to double-check whether we could travel round the sheer rocks which formed the eastern side of the plateau and descended into the lake. I think he also wanted to burnish his reputation as a fisherman by hugging the lake and fishing at the end of the day. But neither a passable route nor a boost to his fishing skills occurred. After three abortive attempts it was clear there was no way around the plateau via the lake. A rough night spent on the rocks and an empty fisherman's swag bag gave him, and us, the clear message we had to go over the top.

Next day we camped half-way up the northern side of the plateau, following a route we had chosen for ourselves. That night we were all immensely grateful for the tarpaulin. The long-threatened rains came with a vengeance and we crawled into our respective hyena holes (smelly, damp and dirty) under the propped-up canvas and attempted to sleep. A damp, rough night but in the morning we rejoiced. Our water supplies were very low and we had all vowed to avoid lake water except *in extremis*. Seven hours of steady rain ensured that our plastic buckets and containers were filled to overflowing with about 90 pints of pure, fresh rainwater. Neither man nor beast was going to go thirsty.

The following night when we were further up the side of the plateau and almost on the top another heavy rain came and lasted until 1.00 p.m. in the afternoon. The going was painfully slow. When we at last reached the top of the plateau we saw it was strewn with thousands of different sized rocks of black lava varying in size from a hen's egg to a football, which shifted dangerously as we crossed over them.

There was absolutely no vegetation whatsoever poking through this insecure lethal black mass. In spite of this, some early expeditions had found the East African oryx (*Oryx beisa*), lesser kudu (*Tragelaphus imberbis),* and ostrich (*Struthio camelus*) near the plateau, species which were not to be found in the wider Turkana basin.

In spite of this hostile, uncompromising environment, and much to my surprise, we passed a Turkana herdsman with some scrawny goats and sheep. The poor fellow told us 40 of his goats had died after the heavy rains of the previous two nights. Josh told me that this often happens when heavy rains come after a prolonged drought and they frequently experienced this on Ol Maisor. We picked our way over this treacherous surface and pitched our camp on top of the plateau at about 3.30 p.m., having set out that day at 6.00 a.m. Fortunately it was a rain-free night "on the rocks".

7th April 2006

My journal:

We covered only about 10 miles today but it was very taxing. After descending from the top of the plateau we entered the steep-sided Mugurr dry river valley. After climbing up its lava-strewn bank, we entered another river valley only to then descend into a third one where the river was full of fast-flowing water. Then we began a three-hour steep and treacherous descent. It was extremely difficult for the camels. There was no track and both the rocks and the lava were formidable. At times our camel boys had to shift huge sharp-edged rocks with their bare hands to enable our camels to pass. Most of the way, in the absence of a guide, we were pioneering our own route. Our camels suffered from cuts to the feet and one unfortunately slipped and fell. Luckily no damage was done. At about 4.00 p.m., 12 hours after setting off, we at last reached the shore of Lake Turkana. There was great jubilation. The team had reached the campsite called Nangal where they had camped after coming out of the Suguta valley on their way to the rendezvous with Jasper and myself in the Sirima Lugga. The circumambulation of the lake had almost been completed.

Next day we rested. All of us, and especially the camels, were exhausted.

In 1888, when the Count Teleki, von Höhnel expedition discovered Lake Turkana, Teleki gave his name to a highly active volcano just to the east of an ancient barrier of lava which cuts off the Suguta Valley from Lake Turkana and is known to this day as The Barrier. It was through the tortuous and treacherous Suguta Valley and over The Barrier that Josh and Ivan had trekked with their camels, friends and camel boys to rendezvous with me at the outset in the Sirima dry riverbed.

Wide streams of solidified lava flow down to the lake from The Barrier, one the colour of milk chocolate, the other almost black. They flow in some places to the lake's edge and close to the dramatic and extinct volcano called Nabayaton, which is situated, distinctively, on the southern edge of the lake. I had climbed Nabayaton on an earlier trek, which I had made with camels through the northern sector of the Suguta Valley, but had then thought it wiser not to clamber into its huge circular cone.

To this day, Nabayaton stands out as a magnificent landmark but Teleki's volcano has seemingly disappeared. What has happened in the intervening 140 years since its "discovery" is a mystery. In an article in the Royal Geographical Society's journal in April 1898, ten years after Teleki's "discovery", it was stated by a Mr. H.S.H. Cavendish that:

> On arriving at the south end of the lake I was surprised to find that Teleki's volcano had entirely disappeared, its place being taken by an entirely flat plain of lava. We got hold of some of the Ligob-men [*El Molo*] who live at the south end of Lake Rudolf and within a couple of miles of the volcano, who told us that about six months ago the lake overflowed and as the waters rushed towards the mountain, the native name of which is Looburura [*Teleki's volcano*], there was a vast explosion, after which the waters swept in where the crater had been and put out the fire.

Mr. Cavendish failed to find Teleki's volcano although he alleged to have discovered another volcano in *"a smoking condition"*.

His Ligob-men, the El Molo, live at the southernmost part of the lake. They are clustered near an island, which before the lake receded had, in Teleki's day, been one of a group of three. A derelict and hostile place, its shades of black, brown and yellow contrast sharply with the jade green tones of the lake. Von Höhnen described their dwellings as *"primitive hay-shaped huts made of stones and grass."* This island is the last resort of the El Molo people.

Numbering less than 100, they are on the verge of extinction as a pure tribal entity, and eke out their existence with a life based on fishing, exporting the sun-dried fish to nearby markets.

*The El Molo love telling a story about a Turkana hunter who caught a hippo in a most unusual way.*

Their origins are undocumented but it is clear that they have survived in their lakeside fastness for centuries and co-existed peacefully with their warring neighbours over a long period of time. The opening of a military station at nearby Loiyangalani over 110 years ago by the British brought new influences to bear on the El Molo. They learnt about trade and some took to becoming pastoralists. We encountered two of them carefully placing sun-dried fish in neat formations on the rocks. In a few years they may well have disappeared, having intermarried with their neighbours.

A Mr. A. M. Champion, gave a lecture to the Royal Geographical Society on the 7th of January, 1935, and stated that:

> The volcano when discovered was in such activity that Teleki had perforce to make his way round the southern side as he was unable to cross the stream of molten lava which enveloped its northern and eastern sides, and extends for a distance of 5 miles to the shore of the lake. Whilst his caravan was making this arduous detour he made a valiant attempt to reach the summit, but was driven back by the fumes emanating from long fissures, which rent the mountainside and rendered further progress impossible. He makes mention of some natives inhabiting the vicinity called the Lokob who would appear to be fisherfolk from several of the surrounding tribes now spoken of as the El Molo, who having lost through disease or raids such stock as they possessed were compelled to eke out a living by catching the fish which abound in the lake.

Mr. Champion made the interesting point in the course of his lecture that the Suguta Valley at 1200 to 1300 feet above sea level made it the lowest point in the whole of the Rift Valley, which extends from Lakes Naivasha and Baringo all the way northwards to Ethiopia and the Red Sea.

Lastly, in 1921, Mr. Barton, a District Officer, says he was told terrifying stories by the Turkana of a mountain of fire and saw at nights a flare in the sky, which gave support to their statements.

Whatever actually has happened, the remains of Teleki's volcano are exceedingly difficult to find and it is certainly not smoking. Nor are other smoking fissures or active volcanos to be found.

It is just to the east of Nabayaton that the remains of a light aircraft can be seen. There were no fatalities and the plane crashed on account of the turbulent and ever-changing wind. It is now greatly reduced in size as Turkana women continue to hack off pieces of metal from the plane in order to fashion a fetching and much prized line of jewellery.

The final trek over the multi-coloured lava, which separates Nabayaton from the remains of Teleki's volcano, was another excruciating one for the camels. And then finally we came to the shore of the lake and managed to buy and slaughter a flat-tailed sheep. Our lucky mascot Fatima that had followed or been carried on a camel's back three-quarters of the way around the lake looked on in horror as the carcass of her fellow creature was hung up on the branch of a tree.

I parted company with the team when Josh's father, John Perrett, met me at a place called Parkati, not far from the Sirima Lugga dry river where six weeks earlier I had started off on the 460-mile-trek around the lake. It was strange to be back in a vehicle, covering in no time distances that would have taken hours by camel. I was yet again struck at how we live today in a frantic rhythm which is entirely alien to the natural rhythm of life. With our ability to cover huge distances in a short space of time we have destroyed our natural rhythm. Only when having spent weeks walking or trekking with a horse or a camel does one recover the pace at which our forebears lived their entire lives.

I finally met up with Jasper at Ol Maisor. "Well done," he said shaking my hand, "so you didn't croak, have a whisk [whisky]."

I realise I have been very fortunate. My first major trek into the African bush, non-motorised and on horseback, took place in May 1957. Since then I have undertaken countless expeditions and treks on horse, camel or on foot in West and East Africa, and in Mongolia and northwest China. In Central Asia I was seeking to protect the critically endangered wild camel. In West Africa I was travelling in the course of my job as a District Officer. In East Africa it was a means of exploring the former Northern Frontier District and to generate additional publicity for the wild camel. My last substantial trek was in the Lop Nur desert, Xingjiang, China in 2011.

I have had many escapades, escapes and adventures and used up my cat's nine lives. I am now playing in extra time. We discovered Kum Su, an unmapped fresh water spring in the salt water Desert of Lop in China; Sengri, a previously undiscovered village in the Alantika Mountains in Northern Nigeria; and a naïve population of wildlife, which had never before seen man, in an unexplored area in Lop Nur. I have worked with people of many tribal cultures and religions in desert and bush.

I was allowed to go into Lop Nur which had been a closed area to foreigners and to local people for 45 years because it was (and in part still is) a nuclear test site. I travelled in a remote mountainous area, the Alantika Mountains on the Nigeria/ Cameroun border, and stayed for three months with the restive and unruly Koma people. This area was closed to any government official, missionary or any other visitor except a District Officer, because of the Koma's propensity to shoot poison-tipped arrows when they saw a stranger approaching their remote territory.

Above all, on countless treks, I have managed to leave western civilisation behind and enter what I would describe as the real world, areas of primitivism, beauty, aridity and supreme challenge – and for this I am profoundly grateful.

The words I wrote after my very first excursion into the Northern Nigeria bush in 1957, aged 22, are still pertinent and convey something of the sheer joy of riding out and discovering the vastness of an unspoilt world for the very first time:

> There was a chill in the air as we rode out of Gombe before the sun had risen on my first trek into the African bush. The suffused light of a waning moon illuminated pools of water in the riverbed. Towering tamarind, locust bean and baobab trees were scattered upon a sward that looked like a lawn in the moonlight.

Dawn broke with a rapidly reddening glow as the sun rose over sugar-loaf-shaped Bima Hill far to our right. It was a dawn of rosy sun-gilded rocks, dappled earth and sparkling dew-dropped bushes and fronds. As the sun rose higher in the bright blue sky, the dew vaporised and wisps of mist faded in quick succession. For about 40 minutes the vigour of the fresh new day filled my lungs, then the freshness evaporated and the air became stagnant in the shimmering heat of an unremitting sun.

Cocks began crowing, people stirred in their huts and the blue smoke of cooking fires drifted up in the early morning haze. Greetings were shouted back and forth. As we slowly moved away, the farms gave way to scrubby acacia bush with bold hills outlined on either side.

I cantered on ahead, pausing to let the carriers catch up and then pushed on again over gullies and dry riverbeds savouring for the very first time the liberated feeling of riding into the vast empty space of Africa.

# PART TWO
# DAM AND BE DAMNED

*Photograph of the construction of the Gibe III dam*

# Dam and be Damned

*"How is it possible that the most intellectual creature ever to walk the planet Earth is destroying its only home?"*

Dr Jane Goodall DBE, Jane Goodall Institute

Since our expedition in 2006 around Lake Turkana a calamitous situation has arisen. The Dassenech who live in the Omo Delta and the Bodi, Hamar, Karo, Kwegu and Mursi tribes whose tribal lands embrace the river to the north, have been evicted from their ancestral lands. They are no longer able to farm in the way their forebears farmed for millennia.

Centuries of collective wisdom relating to livestock, bi-annual flood-dependent cultivation, and complex tribal customs in harmony with the environment have cruelly and ruthlessly been obliterated. All this has happened in the fourteen years since our pioneering trek around the lake with camels.

And not only the Omo Delta and the Omo riverine area in Ethiopia have been affected. Lake Turkana's water level is falling dramatically and 100,000 people who live around or near the lake are short of food.

What has happened?

The Ethiopian government is transforming more than 926,000 acres of the lower Omo River into industrial plantations. Vast areas of land adjacent to the west bank of the Omo River have been designated for growing sugar and cotton. This land is vital agricultural and grazing land for the tribal people. The first of four planned sugar-processing factories started production in early 2017. In addition, organic cotton projects and the removal of indigenous populations with attendant human rights abuses have occurred.

The Omo Valley Farm Corporation is a 24,700 acre cotton farm, of which 11,366 acres is let to a Turkish Company, the Else Textile Group, to grow organic cotton on an industrial scale. The 24,700 acres were originally in an Ethiopian Government protected area; but this status was "de-gazetted" or rescinded in 2011 by the Government in order that cotton could be grown.

ICEA, the Global Organic Textile Standard organisation, based in Italy, backs up the figures above: it has certified that Else Textile's organic cotton cultivation is indeed farmed on 11,366 acres of the Omo Valley Farm land. It confirms that the corporation acquired 24,700 acres from the government of Ethiopia.

Yet no mention is made of the tribal people who were living on the land, whose livelihood was destroyed and whose rights were ignored when the "de-gazetting" – the removal of its official status by publishing it in a government gazette – took place.

To make way for these commercial plantations and factories, tens of thousands of hectares of land have been expropriated and thousands of local people permanently displaced, reportedly without adequate prior consultation or compensation.

But far worse is the Gibe Dam Project, the construction of a cascade of five huge dams on the Omo River to generate electricity. Gibe III, the tallest dam in Africa at 800 feet, was opened in December 2016.

However, there is a disastrous and irretrievable price to pay across the border. The water level in Lake Turkana is dropping rapidly and the end result in a few years' time could be devastating. The lake could split in two because of the fall in the water level, which would result in the southern half of the lake having minimal fresh water source.

A literate Turkana wrote to me in 2017, "The Lake Turkana shore line has shrunk, the salinity of the lake water has increased and it is now not drinkable for man or animals. Fish numbers have gone down and this means no staple food and therefore starvation and death."

This has occurred without any meaningful consultation with the tribal communities affected. The state has appropriated grazing lands and freshwater, threatening the tribal peoples' vital resources and local heritage.

Most importantly, the completion of Gibe III has eliminated the twice-yearly flood on which the agriculturalists were dependent, and radically reduced the Omo River's flow, which produces 90 per cent of Lake Turkana's freshwater input. In doing so, it has reduced sediments and nutrients essential for traditional agriculture, riverside pastures and fish habitat. Scientists call it flood-retreat agriculture. As a swollen river blankets a dry plain and then recedes, it replenishes the thin soil with enough nutrients to sprout grass for cattle and allow the cultivation of crops like corn and sorghum. It's an approach that indigenous groups have been practising for centuries around the world, allowing them to subsist in arid and otherwise marginal climates.

Over 30 per cent of the lake inflow from Ethiopia has been diverted for commercial irrigation projects. The result could be a fall in the lake level comparable to that of Central Asia's Aral Sea, on the Kazakh–Uzbek border, formerly the fourth largest lake in the world, which has shrunk by over two-thirds since the 1960s. The whole area has been turned into desert – because of irrigation abstraction by the Russians to grow cotton – resulting in "the world's worst environmental disaster".

All of this has occurred despite the Omo Delta Region being designated in 1980 a UNESCO World Heritage Site. As Richard Leakey, the Kenyan paleoanthropologist, conservationist and former politician put it with a remarkable degree of under-statement, "these happenings are profoundly disturbing."

It is much more than "profoundly disturbing", it is an unmitigated tragedy.

There is another extremely important medical reason why tribes in the Omo Delta, who have remained untouched for centuries, should not be violently uprooted. Roughly 99 per cent of man's evolutionary history occurred in Africa. Modern humans emerged there 200,000 years ago. About 100,000 years later small groups of our collective ancestors began a procreational march across the world. They took with them a fraction of our genetic diversity. As people in Africa intermarried and reproduced, that diversity remained and was transformed by environmental pressures and disease. "Tapping into this diversity has huge implications for all humanity," Matthew Nelson, head of genetics at GlaxoSmithKline, stated. "If I was able to access a full medical history of 500,000 people across five countries in Africa, and analyse the resulting genetic data, that would be a far better investment in understanding genes and disease than a 500,000 person study in Europe."

Without robust data from remote African populations, scientists are missing out on the secrets of thousands of generations of human evolution – and the tribes around Lake Turkana and in the Omo Delta live directly in what is called, "the Cradle of Mankind".

The Bodi, Hamar, Karo, Kwegu and Mursi tribes rely on the natural flood cycles of the Omo River for their sustainable practices of flood-recession farming, fishing and livestock grazing. Like generations of their forebears, they plant sorghum, maize and beans in the riverside soils after the yearly flood, relying on the moisture and nutrient-rich sediment the Omo deposits each year.

With the filling of the Gibe III reservoir, water hasn't reached the tribes' riverside lands, curtailing harvests and grazing. Desperate to find grass, herders have moved their cattle into the Mago National Park, 485 miles south of Addis Ababa and north of a large 90 per cent bend in the Omo River, which has unleashed fighting with government soldiers charged with protecting the park and its wildlife.

The Ethiopian government views the Gibe III Dam, now owned and administered by the national company Ethiopian Electric Power, as essential to its economic advancement. The dam rises 797 feet, can hold back 3,233.5 billion gallons of water, and has a planned hydropower capacity of 1,870 megawatts, far in excess of Ethiopian projected consumption. Electricity generation has already begun.

The reservoir-filling process has reduced inflow into the lake by two-thirds since 2016. But even after the reservoir is full, flows into Lake Turkana will be reduced by the diversion of Omo River water for industrial scale irrigated agriculture. Without the river's yearly supply, Lake Turkana is steadily losing water, because evaporation losses are no longer being balanced by inflows.

Everything changed in 2015 when a government-backed Italian firm, Salini Impregilo, the country's largest construction and infrastructure giant based in Milan, completed the Gibe III hydroelectric dam upriver – a project for which there was no competitive bidding. All seasonal flooding ceased for the first time in millennia. Famine ensued.

Simultaneously, water was diverted for a government scheme to establish industrial sugar-cane plantations throughout the Omo Valley. The new irrigation system soon became a breeding ground for malarial mosquitoes. Foreign workers brought illnesses of their own, including HIV, into the once-isolated region. As the coronavirus pandemic intensifies in Africa, and Ethiopia has enforced few precautions, it seems inevitable that the virus will reach these tribes as well. The total number of deaths from illness has been difficult to establish due to the semi-nomadic lifestyle of these tribal people, as well as a strong local taboo against naming the dead. The people, however, insist that deaths have been "many".

Recent major cutbacks in size and processing capacity cast doubt on the economic returns of the state-owned Kuraz Sugar Development Project (KSDP) in Ethiopia's lower Omo Valley. However, it is not certain whether the KSDP will be able to meet the great expectations placed on its contributions to the national economy, but rather how much this unprecedented agri-business venture will fall short of its stated agro-economic and macro-economic objectives.

The upstream damming of the Omo River, which allows for the development of irrigated sugar-cane cultivation, has ruled out the continuation of flood-recession agriculture – the central pillar of indigenous livelihoods in the Omo Valley. Although clearly unparalleled in terms of its impact on the local environmental and social landscape, the status of central aspects of the KSDP remain uncontested.

People who depend on fishing for their livelihood said that their daily catch from the lake has been reduced. One 50-year-old woman living near Lake Turkana told Human Rights Watch in August 2016: "It has been difficult these days … the main issue has been hunger. There is reduced water in the lake."

While multiple factors contribute to the decline, including overfishing and unsustainable fishing practices, a drop in lake levels will most likely reduce catches even further.

The Kenyan government has done little to address the impact from Ethiopia's Omo Valley development, or to press Ethiopia to take steps to mitigate the damage and to consult with and inform affected communities about the impact of the project. Why? Because Kenya will benefit from the electricity that Gibe III will generate – electricity which is far in excess of Ethiopia's own requirements.

"What am I going to eat?" a man of the Mursi tribe told Human Rights Watch. "They said to take all my cattle and to sell them and to only tie one up at my house. What can I do with only one? I am a Mursi. If hunger comes I shoot a cow's neck and drink blood. If we sell them all for money how will we eat?"

According to Ethiopia's Growth and Transformation Plan, the government has identified sugar production as one of the cornerstones for increasing the country's competitive advantage in the agro-processing subsector. By 2021, it is expected to have 13 large sugar factories, yet sugar, like cotton, is a non-sustainable crop.

China, which is financing this sugar factory development, sees things totally differently as this *People's Daily* newspaper report in 2017 shows:

## CHINESE COMPANY WORKS ON ENERGY-EFFICIENT NEW FACTORY, BRINGING JOBS AND HOPE TO AN IMPOVERISHED REGION

In Ethiopia, the construction of new giant sugar factories is in full swing. There are now 10 such plants being built, and among them is Omo-Kuraz 5 in the southern Omo region. This is the largest and is being built by a private company from China.

Jiangxi Jianglian International Engineering, a company with headquarters in Nanchang, Jiangxi province [eastern China], won the engineering, procurement and construction contract in 2013.

Construction work started in 2015 and is 5 per cent complete, with sugar-making machines arriving from China. According to the company, the first phase of the project is scheduled for completion by November next year.

On completion, "the project will increase Ethiopia's annual refined sugar production by 600,000 tons," says Huang Fu, the company's general manager for the project. "It will no doubt help stimulate economic growth in the country."

"Our production capacity had not been over 400,000 metric tons before. But now, due to the expansion of the present factories and the new ones that will become fully operational this year, the nation will have the capacity to produce 700,000 tons of sugar this year," says Gashaw Aychlum, corporate communication CEO of Ethiopian Sugar Corp, as quoted by The Ethiopian Herald.

"The nation is planning to export sugar, starting in the coming fiscal year. We could say the nation is in a state of 'sugar development revolution.' "

Jiangxi Jianglian International Engineering entered the Ethiopian sugar market in 2013, says Yuan Jialin, the then-team leader for bidding. In order to stand a chance of participating in the bidding, Yuan says he spent a great deal of time persuading Ethiopian Sugar Corporation, the owner of the project.

The company's strengths in recycling technology helped it stand out. The Omo area, where the project is located, is a barren land and the project's power supply was the biggest problem.

According to the company's proposal, on completion the factory will generate power by burning of sugar-cane bagasse, the pulpy fibrous material left over when sugar has been extracted. At the same time, the waste sugar molasses produced as a by-product will be used to make alcohol, and ash from the burning will be used to fertilize sugar-cane fields.

The $647 million project has broken records as the largest-ever overseas deal achieved in Jiangxi province.

Many saw us as a dark horse," Yuan says. "In fact, this success is the result of our long-term endeavour, following the government's encouragement to go global and the Belt and Road Initiative." [*The Belt and Road Initiative is a global development strategy adopted by the Chinese government in 2013 involving infrastructure development and investments in nearly 70 countries and international organisations.*]

Building a single sugar factory is like building a town, CEO Aychlum says. With rapid development, new sugar projects in Ethiopia are being located in remote areas instead of being concentrated in one region.

The Omo-Kuraz 5 plant is 1,000 km from the capital, Addis Ababa, at an altitude of 2,500 metres, an area identified as most suitable for sugar-cane growing and production. The area lacks infrastructure and services. It takes two days to travel there from the capital, due to the lack of highways and railways. The area lacks water, which locals have to transport for long distances.

When the company kicked off the project in 2015, the first thing it did was to drill wells.

"We dug two wells – one for the construction work and one for locals. It is all free," says Huang.

According to the company, it has employed about 300 Ethiopians in construction, earning an average income of 3,000 *birr* ($129) a month. That is close to the salary paid to local bank staff. When the factory is in full operation, it will create about 1,000 jobs in the plant itself and another 12,000 seasonal jobs on the plantations.

A construction worker from Addis Ababa, who gave his name as Getachew, says he is happy to get a job with a Chinese company. "I never worked on construction sites before. It is great that I could get training from the company, and now I have become a skilled worker, adept at working with steel bars."

Representatives of Ethiopian Sugar Corporation also speak

highly of the Chinese company. "In my experience with the Chinese enterprises, the company has the best management. It abides by the construction plans rigidly and tolerates no mistakes," says Ekalh, a project manager.

"Ethiopia is Africa's second-most populous nation, with a mostly young population of about 100 million. It hopes its investments will meet the demands of the job market and keep the nation stable and prosperous. The contribution from Chinese companies is massive and highly visible across the country. Ethiopia attracted foreign investment of $1.2 billion in the first six months of the 2016-17 fiscal year, dominated by Chinese companies, according to the Ethiopian Investment Commission."

Chinese involvement in mega projects in a developing country can quickly turn that country into a financial vassal of China. For example, every time Sri Lanka's former president, Mahinda Rajapaksa, turned to his Chinese allies for loans and assistance with an ambitious port project, the answer was, "yes", though feasibility studies said the port wouldn't be economic.

After years of construction and renegotiation with China Harbour Engineering Company, one of Beijing's largest state-owned enterprises, the Hambantota Port Development Project distinguished itself by failing, as predicted. With tens of thousands of ships passing by along one of the world's busiest shipping lanes, the port drew only 34 ships in 2012.

Sri Lanka lies right on China's primary supply route of crude oil from the Middle East and Africa. Sri Lanka was to become a major hub along the 21st Century Maritime Silk Road, a series of interconnected, Chinese-run-invested ports stretching from the Yangtze and Pearl River Deltas through Southeast Asia, across the Indian Ocean, up the coast of Africa, and through the Suez Canal to Greece.

Sri Lanka's government struggled to make payments on the debt incurred for both the port and a new international airport, constructed in Mr Rajapaska's home area and which is now redundant. Under heavy pressure and after months of negotiations, with the Chinese, the government handed over the port and 15,000 acres of land around it to the Chinese on a 99-year-lease.

A very different picture of the sugar and cotton development in Ethiopia was outlined by The Oakland Institute, a progressive think tank based in Oakland, California and founded in 2004 by Anuradha Mittal, the former co-director of Food First. Mittal is considered an "expert on trade, development, human rights, democracy, and agriculture issues".

In 2017 it released a report based on field research in the Lower Omo Valley between September 2017 and May 2018. It confirms the disastrous effect of these two projects on three of the indigenous groups of the region: the Bodi, Mursi and Northern Kwegu. The ending of the Omo River's flood has wiped out local livelihoods.

Initial promises made by the government and the Italian construction company Salini Impregilo, responsible for building the dam, that an artificial flood would be released have never materialised. Today, these communities face acute hunger, displacement of livelihoods, and the eradication of their culture and identities.

The Ethiopian government has pressured the tribal people to abandon pastoralism and adopt sedentary lifestyles. But resettlement sites offered for this purpose have been riddled with failed promises and corruption. Plots are often not big enough to feed families, ripened crops have been ploughed over, communities have been forced to dig their own irrigation canals under hazardous conditions, and key services that were promised – schooling, healthcare, grinding mills, food aid and electricity – have either failed to materialise or been woefully inadequate.

As with many so-called development projects, the KSDP came with the promise of hundreds of thousands of new jobs in the region. But only a small percentage of this employment has actually been created and most has been given to migrant workers from other regions of the country. This is rapidly changing demographics in the region, making the indigenous peoples minorities in their own ancestral lands. The jobs that have been offered to the Bodi, Mursi and Northern Kwegu involve hunting buffalo that eat the sugar-cane and removing crushed sugar-cane refuse. The jobs are mostly seasonal, temporary and low paid.

Survival International's Director, Stephen Corry said:

Salini has ignored crucial evidence, made false promises and ridden roughshod over the rights of hundreds of thousands of people. Thousands are now facing starvation because Italy's largest contractor, and one of its best-known companies, didn't think human rights were worth its time. The real consequences of the Ethiopian government's devastating policies for its country's "development", which are shamefully supported by western aid agencies like the UK's DFID and USAID, are plain for all to see. Stealing people's land and causing massive environmental destruction is not "progress", it is a death sentence for tribal peoples.

And of course, this is not white colonialism or neo-colonialism. It is, to put it crudely, black on black.

In the face of these changes, hunger is widespread. Food aid that was initially used to draw local communities to resettlement sites has been used to coerce people to stay in those sites.

The impacts of this developmental "transformation" are reflected in the words of a Mursi elder:

This is terrible. If the flood had come, we would be at the Omo now catching fish. But we are now sitting in the plains with nothing to eat ... Death is near.

This is Oakland's fourth report on South Omo. In 2013 it accused the Ethiopian government of using killings, beatings and rapes in order to force indigenous communities to accept the sugar-cane projects. It also accused western aid agencies of covering up evidence of the abuses.

International groups – Human Rights Watch, Survival International and the Friends of Lake Turkana – have been outspoken in their condemnation of the Ethiopian government for this continuing abuse in South Omo.

The Oakland Institute reported that Desalegn Tekle Loyale, a doctoral student at Addis Ababa University who grew up in the valley, said the government did not engage with local communities before commencing the project.

"None of us have been consulted," he said. "We just heard the dam had already started – nothing else."

Benedikt Kamski, a doctoral researcher at the University of Freiburg's Arnold Bergstraesser Institute, said previous opportunities to mitigate some of the project's harmful impacts had been side-lined by the government.

"Setbacks in the project led to a certain rethinking within the Sugar Corporation concerning the implementation and how local communities should be involved," he asserted. "However, financial bottlenecks, political pressure, and above all the government's vision of development seem to have prevented a change of course."

Despite criticism, Abiy Ahmed's administration has pledged to finalise the sugar projects. In October 2018, at the inauguration of Omo-Kuraz III Sugar Factory, the prime minister said earlier problems had been "alleviated" and spoke of a need "to march forward".

The Ethiopian Minister of Water, Irrigation and Energy, Dr. Seleshi Bekele, asserted it would be wrong to assume, "the traditional way of living was great and had no problems".

He added that, "irrigated agriculture is more advantageous because it can produce up to three harvests per year."

Yet there are some signs of a change in approach.

In April 2019 at a seminar on South Omo's livelihood challenges, held in Addis Ababa, government minister Seyoum Mesfin Gebredingel told visiting academics and journalists that the new government recognised certain "development interventions in the pastoralist areas … came with a cost."

The minister cited, in particular, "megaprojects like Gibe III" and added that the government, "will not allow a repeat of those situations."

"Since Abiy came to power researchers are being treated differently, especially with regards to information sharing," said Kamski. "This is indeed a promising development and should be taken as a cue for instigating constructive dialogue and the joint development of mitigation measures."

Others are proposing ways to soften the impact of Gibe III.

"All options should be on the table in terms of sharing the benefits from these projects," said Jed Stevenson, an anthropologist at Durham University, who suggested wider access to irrigation for local communities, as well as schemes allowing them a share of the profits from crops grown on plantations.

Meanwhile, some have continued to call for controlled release of flood waters from the dam, at least until local people are able to move away from their traditional livelihoods – although experts have warned this would mean a significant loss in hydropower revenue.

"For the communities there is no other solution [besides] a serious release of the dam," said Claudia Carr, Associate Professor at Berkeley University, and a specialist in water resources and river basin environments. "There's just nothing else."

Dams can create serious and unforeseen problems. In July 2020, China had to blow up a dam on the Chu River, a subsidiary of the Yangtze River in Anhui Province inland from Shanghai, after continual heavy rains caused severe flooding and landslides killing over 150 people. Approximately 1.8 million people have been evacuated and there is concern that other cities may have to be evacuated. The cost of destruction is estimated at £5 billion. This quantity of rainfall was not anticipated in the modelling for this dam.

And now Ethiopia is engaged in a bitter dispute with Egypt over its new Renaissance Dam. The dam's effect on the Nile, Egypt's lifeline and Africa's longest river, is unknown. The Nile and its routine flooding provide rich sediment for 90 per cent of

Egyptian agriculture and as with the Omo River, this has occurred for centuries. Egypt realises the potential of the Renaissance Dam to give Ethiopia the power to control the Nile's flow. This could cause widespread famine. Egypt is currently considering military options including blowing up this dam. While the Sudan might receive electricity from this dam its agriculture could also be affected.

Hydroelectric power stations do not consume water, but the speed with which a dam's reservoir is filled will affect the flow downstream, as is happening with the diminished Omo River's flow into Lake Turkana.

Lake Turkana Wind Power Project (LTWP), the wind power development on the eastern shore of Lake Turkana, is the single largest investment in Kenya's history.

The wind farm covers 40,000 acres and is located in Loiyangalani District, in Marsabit County, approximately 339 miles by road, north of Nairobi.

The 70 billion Kenya shillings wind farm has a capacity of 310 MW, enough to supply one million homes. It comprises 365 wind turbines, each with a capacity of 850 kilowatts; the associated overhead electric grid distribution system and a high voltage substation connect it to the national grid. The power produced is bought at a fixed price by Kenya Power (KPLC) over a 20-year period in accordance with the Power Purchase Agreement (PPA). The project was completed in January 2017; however, the line evacuating the power generated was not completed until July 2019.

Yet again, the local people were not adequately consulted when their land was acquired.

Lake Turkana Wind Power – like many companies making large-scale land acquisitions in Africa – benefited from historically weak legislation protecting communal land. The now defunct Marsabit County Council leased the land to them with minimal local discussion. A court case was eventually opened alleging that the land was leased illegally. The judgment given on the 25th April 2018 proclaimed the issues raised, "are of great public importance and of great public interest, are weighty, complex and will require a substantial amount of time to conduct the trial. The matter deserves the constitution of a Bench of Judges for hearing and determination." In other words, the case will drag on long after the project is completed.

Much of the corporate narrative around the wind farm suggests it is bringing development to a previously empty area and one which requires investment. But this belies a more complex past. Turkana, Rendille and Samburu tribes people lived on the concession land and shared – frequently fought over – its resources.

The concession is the location of the Rendille tribe's initiation ceremony, which takes place every 14 years and signifies the transition of young people into adulthood. A Samburu clan also traces its origins to a water pool within the concession. Ironically, the area is not connected to the national grid so the people who live on the land will not benefit from cheap energy.

Although the project is not as damaging to the local people as are the Gibe dams, the cotton, sugar plantations and the factories in Ethiopia, it has destroyed forever the wilderness, isolation and savage beauty of Lake Turkana.

I frequently seem to have undertaken journeys in remote parts of Africa or Central Asia, or lived for some years in a barely accessible part of Africa, just before "development" arrived and the people and the place were irrevocably changed.

For example, my experience living for two years in tribally diverse Tangale-Waja and four years on the extremely remote Mambilla Plateau in Northern Nigeria where there was no road, and a large percentage of the population had never seen a vehicle. I worked there just before the road to the top of the plateau was completed.

My extreme good fortune was in being able to enter Lop Nur seven times, the uninhabited former nuclear test area of China, in search of the critically endangered wild camel, when it was 58,000 square miles of totally undeveloped desert – apart from the blight of radiation. Today, Chinese sensitivities related to their treatment of the resident Uighur population, which surrounds Lop Nur, means that the Desert of Lop is once again out of bounds for foreigners.

My crossing of the Sahara on a camel from Lake Chad to Tripoli in 2001–2002 just a few years before Boko Haram, and other militant terrorist agencies linked to Isis, were active in Niger and Nigeria, and Libya became awash with fanatical Islamic factions and modern weaponry.

And now our journey with camels around Lake Turkana only a few short years before the onset of irrevocable and destructive "development". Development, which has changed for ever, not only the people but a landscape which is known as the "cradle of mankind" because of the paleoanthropological discoveries at Koobi Fora near Lake Turkana.

I always have been *laudator temporis acti*, a lover of times past, and I am instinctively resistant to change. I have repeated Alexander Pope's lines over and over to myself since I was a boy, "Be not the first by whom the new are tried, Nor yet the last to lay the old aside." Resistance to change frequently comes in an individual's declining years but with me it came at an early age. I always wanted the Indian to topple the Cowboy.

It upsets me to see development and extreme change in an area which has largely remained the same for centuries or even millennia. I know progress cannot be stopped, but abrupt and irrevocable change can be deeply regrettable. Regrettable because ancient cultures and traditions cannot stand up to, or resist, the onslaught of a more powerful culture.

It was ever thus. So busy are we ruthlessly exploiting this world and its primitive inhabitants we do not stop to think what we are really doing. After this comes the so-called benevolence – religious, political, economic, scientific, medical and technological. Like lava from Teleki's volcano it will flow over tribal man: a creeping, choking layer of civilisation, which will bury him forever. Primitive people can exist only in their tribal culture and lands. They cannot be preserved because we know how to preserve only one kind of thing – a dead thing.

I know the rural rustic's existence and the life of the "primitive" native can frequently be one of hunger, deprivation, deep superstition and fear. Life can for the primitive be "nasty, brutish and short," in Thomas Hobbes's telling phrase. But Hobbes's quotation describes a society without rules of governance, and tribal societies have complex tribal rules of governance which every member of the tribe understands.

Once change enters into a traditional society, be it via a radio, television or a mobile phone, the traditional way of life is doomed.

A nostalgic longing for times past can be easily demolished, and no argument can hope to sustain it in its entirety. And I am fully aware that as the world moves rapidly forward you cannot keep tribal people locked into traditional societies as if they were animals in a zoo. I am also aware that some traditional societies are evil and prey on their neighbours in obscene and abominable ways.

But when the inevitable change comes it should be conducted humanely. Alien religions should not be forced on people, their artefacts should not be destroyed by religious zealots. All too frequently unsophisticates are dragged into an alien world, dispossessed of their land and rights and offered no adequate compensation. This happens because, as the Hausa people of Northern Nigeria say in a telling phrase: *Ba su da wayo. Idanunsu ba su bude ba* – "they are simple people, their eyes have not been opened."

As I pass through, for example, a modern airport and see the deadening uniformity, which tells you nothing about the country you are in, then I can understand what blanket development in the very broadest and widest sense of the word has cost the human race – its individuality.

Frequently, the core motivation behind "development" is

unmitigated human greed – the deadliest sin of mankind in my opinion.

When the wilderness has all been sold out and the people displaced, then remorse might set in. But it will be too late. What has been obliterated can never be recreated. It cannot be remade as a national park, because gazetted paradises are artificial and imbued with sentimentality.

Man cannot stand still, he is driven to "progress", and the pace of human progression increases year by year – as does the size of the human population. Modern man places implicit belief in his social and economic models. He sees continual prosperity following upon unending economic growth and takes this shibboleth completely for granted – until a coronavirus emerges to puncture what he believed was an absolute truth.

Dr. Jane Goodall asserts:

> It is our disregard for nature and our disrespect of the animals we should share the planet with that has caused this pandemic ... We have to realise we are part of the natural world, we depend on it, and as we destroy it we are actually stealing the future from our children.

In 1973 Alistair Graham and Peter Beard published a remarkable book called *Eyelids of Morning*, which recounts their time researching Lake Turkana's then huge population of 14,000 crocodiles. During the course of their research, they acquired remarkable insights into the mind-set of the Turkana. In their book, Graham made a telling prophecy, which has now come to pass:

> The tranquillity of the Lake Rudolf wilderness will be disturbed because urban industrial "successful" man needs the land and its resources. Therefore he will civilise it. ... The windy distances of Lake Rudolf will be shortened and obscured by roads and planes and hotels and sightseers and fishermen and game wardens and scientists and town planners and all the other conquistadores of the superior civilisation of today and tomorrow,
> Like the American Indian a century ago, the Turkana have

met an intruder which neither their bravest warriors nor their strongest magic can deal with; they have come upon their Manifest Destiny. The Turkana, the crocodiles, the lake and the land – all are about to be rubbed out.

Industrial man, unlike primitive man, rejects the concept of living in harmony with nature. He has the colossal impertinence to think he is utterly in command of the natural world and capable of ordering the destiny of all things. It appears to be the fate of all the great wilderness areas on the planet to be eventually destroyed by technological man.

Leonardo da Vinci in the late fifteenth century was absolutely right when he made a prophecy in *Codex Atlanticus* about the Passing of Paradise:

A countless multitude will sell publicly and without hindrance things of the very greatest value, without licence from the Lord of these things, which were never theirs nor in their power; and human justice will take no account of this.

# APPENDIX 1

# The Giants

*The hunter was a two-footed giant. He towered ten feet above the ground, his arms the thickness of doum palm trunks, his legs even thicker. He was a man of huge dimensions, a giant, but he was human. His intended victim was a rhinoceros, which weighed over a ton. Stealthily the giant man approached his target carrying his weapon – a huge boulder. The rhino was grazing contently, quite oblivious that he was the target of this magnificent man. With silent steps the man approached the rhino from behind and brought the mighty boulder crashing down on his neck. A knife flashed, the rhino's head was severed and raised on high. The hunter drained the blood from the head and drank.*

This Turkana folk tale alludes to a race of giants who lived near the lake and further to the east many millennia ago. These tales of the giants are commonplace and are not confined to the Turkana people, even the Somali have folk tales of a huge race of men who lived on their tribal lands a long time ago. Within all the pastoral tribes of Kenya's far north, old tribal tales and histories are still remembered and handed down orally from one generation to the next. Some fables uniformly tell of a legendary race of giant humans who were capable of Herculean acts of strength, diggers of immense wells and who allegedly lie buried deep beneath the numerous stone cairns found all over the north. Indeed we saw some of these cairns as we passed the eastern shore of Lake Turkana.

The Somalis call these people the Madanle, the Gabbra call them Wardai. As well as stone cairns, these mythical people left behind a huge number of wells, which could only have been dug by people with superior engineering skills. In 1927 a Mr. A.T. Curle excavated a large burial cairn. He discovered an earthenware bowl which when pieced together was of a most unusual design and shape and totally unlike anything the nomadic people used. He commented that, "Its fragility would render it unsuited to a nomadic race."

Later, in 1935, geologist John Parkinson uncovered a cairn in which there were human bones, which he estimated to be those of a man six foot five inches tall. Not a giant by today's standards but certainly a giant when compared to the average stature of native tribes and indeed ourselves millennia ago. Interestingly, a number of the 3,000-year-old mummies dug up in the Gobi desert in Xinjiang Province in China were in excess of six foot five inches. They are reputed to be Celts by some because of the similarity in the weave of their cloth to Celtic weave.

All is speculation, but tribal folklore maintains there was an extremely tall race of men who lived near Lake Turkana and beyond over three thousand years ago.

# APPENDIX 2

# Prince Rudolf

A final word on Prince Rudolf, the friend, fervent supporter and patron of the discoverer of the Jade Sea. Unfortunately, he is much more widely known because of an infamous affair, which resulted in a death pact in the Castle of Mayerling, 20 miles south-west of Vienna. His mistress and partner in the pact, Marie Vetsera, the daughter of a baron, has been portrayed as wholly innocent but it appears she was far from unworldly. Her mother was determined to marry her into the higher echelons of Viennese society. But even her mother thought that an affair with a Crown Prince was a rung too far up society's ladder, especially as the Prince was a married man. Baroness Vetsera felt that such a liaison would ruin the Vetsera family name, and her daughter would be cast forever as an ambitious royal mistress. Long before Marie snuggled up to her princely lover like "a little animal", in one biographer's telling phrase, she had clearly delighted various young men in Viennese society, especially some spirited cavalry officers. But with the Prince, she had found, or so she thought, true love.

As for poor Rudolf, his pious and chilling wife, Stephanie, ignored him and his great beauty of a mother treated him as a child. Meanwhile his father, Emperor Franz Joseph, suspected him of liberal sympathies and of conspiring with radical elements in Hungary who wanted to separate their country from the empire. As a consequence he was kept a virtual prisoner within the restraining bonds of the court and suffered severe depression.

Little wonder that under these family pressures and constraints, he succumbed to the warmth, comforts and delights of the "little animal". Unfortunately, Marie's passionate love could not rid him of the acute depression, which was intensified by an appalling row with his father.

Suffering greatly from the "black dog", he spent the night of 30th January 1889 in a hunting lodge with Marie Vetsera where, as the most commonly accepted version goes, he entered into a suicide pact with his seventeen-year-old mistress so they could forever remain together. She lay before her lover on the bed and he shot her through the forehead. Rudolf did not, however, kill himself until the dawn had broken. He then methodically ordered and ate a leisurely breakfast, calmly picked up a mirror, took careful aim and shot himself.

To avert a great scandal, Marie's relatives were forced to sign a document saying that she had committed suicide and her body was hurriedly spirited away wrapped in a blanket. However, if she had died for true love, her lover quite certainly had not. Before he had left for Mayerling, he had spent several hours with another mistress, Mizzi Kaspar, to whom he left a letter steeped in words of love and everlasting devotion plus a generous amount of money. Just what had been going on in his head we shall never know. We do know that Mizzi had refused to join him in a suicide pact.

After the two deaths, Emperor Franz Joseph ordered the hunting lodge at Mayerling to be razed to the ground and a Catholic convent to be built in its place. It still stands, and the Carmelite nuns there pray daily for the souls of Rudolf and Marie. Moreover, at the centennial mass for Crown Prince Rudolf, all the prayers were said for the Prince. No mention was made of Marie Vetsera.

Rudolf's death changed the succession, and contributed in 1918 to the end of the ancient house of the Habsburgs and their

imperial rule. The removal of the liberal Rudolf made Franz Joseph's conservative policies easier to pursue but Rudolf's sensational death immediately caused a dynastic and indeed a subsequent world crisis.

As Rudolf was the only son of Franz Joseph, the emperor's brother Karl Ludwig became heir presumptive to the Austro-Hungarian Empire. He renounced his succession rights a few days later in favour of his eldest son Franz Ferdinand – the same Archduke Franz Ferdinand of Austria who was subsequently assassinated with his wife Sophie, Duchess of Hohenberg, by one Gavrilo Princip in Sarajevo on 28th June 1914. An event which led directly to the commencement of the First World War.

# Acknowledgements

Jane Goodall DBE, the Life Patron of the Wild Camel Protection Foundation took time out of her extremely busy life to write a generous Foreword for which I am extremely grateful.

Much thanks goes to Kathryn Rae, and Roderic McGregor in England and Amanda Perrett in Kenya who read and re-read the typescript and gave me invaluable advice, and to Josh Perrett, who corrected my geographical memory lapses.

Amanda Helm of Helm Information shaped my typescript into a readable book and advised brilliantly on all the technical aspects of publication. Proof-reader and indexer, John Skermer is also due a hearty round of applause.

Without Josh Perrett and Ivan Jensen, who undertook all the pre-expedition planning and preparation, the successful circumambulation (wonderful word) of the Lake would not have been achieved. They overcame countless difficulties with skill, coolness, competence and good humour and have my heartfelt thanks.

Josh's father, John Perrett spent considerable time on pre- and post-expedition logistics, as did my wise friend and fellow traveller in both the Gobi and Sahara Deserts, the late Jasper Evans.

Lastly many plaudits to the six members of the "Ol Maisor team" and to the 18 wonderful camels without whom nothing could have been accomplished; and to the late Halewijn

Scheurmann, who succeeded in a task which others said was completely impossible – ferrying our camels one by one across the mighty River Omo.

The expedition photographs are the copyright of John Hare, Josh Perrett and Ivan Jensen. All endeavour has been made to obtain copyright permission for the photographs alluding to recent developments in the Omo Delta, on the Omo River and near Lake Turkana.

# Bibliography

Pern, Stephen (1979). *Another Land, Another Sea.*Littlehampton Book Services, Worthing.
Burton, Richard (1856). *Personal Narrative of a Pilgrimage to El-Medinah and Meccah.* Longman, Brown, Green and Longmans, London.
Brown, Monty (1989). *Where Giants Trod: the Saga of Kenya's Desert Lake.* Quiller Press, London.
Hillaby, John (1964). *Journey to the Jade Sea* Constable, London.
Graham, Alistair & Beard, Peter (1973). *Eyelids of Morning: the Mingled Destinies of Crocodiles and Men.* New York Graphic Society, New York.
Höhnel, Ludwig von (1894). *Discoveries of Lakes Rudolf and Stephanie: A Narrative of Count Samuel Teleki's Exploring & Hunting Expedition in Eastern Equatorial Africa in 1887 & 1888.* Longmans Green and Co, London.
Neumann, Arthur (1898). *Elephant Hunting in East Equatorial Africa.* Roland Ward, London.

# Conversion Tables

## Temperature

To convert from Celsius to Fahrenheit, first multiply by 9/5, then add 32.

# Length

| US or Imperial | | Metric |
|---|---|---|
| 1 inch [in] | | 2.54 cm |
| 1 foot [ft] | 12 in | 0.3048 m |
| 1 yard [yd] | 3 ft | 0.9144 m |
| 1 mile | 1760 yd | 1.6093 km |
| 1 int nautical mile | 2025.4 yd | 1.853 km |

# Area

| US or Imperial | | Metric |
|---|---|---|
| 1 sq inch [in²] | | 6.4516 cm² |
| 1 sq foot [ft²] | 144 in² | 0.0929 m² |
| 1 sq yd [yd²] | 9 ft² | 0.8361 m² |
| 1 acre | 4840 yd² | 4046.9 m² |
| 1 sq mile [mile²] | 640 acres | 2.59 km² |

# Volume/Capacity

| US Measure | Imperial | Metric |
|---|---|---|
| 1 cu inch [in³] | | 16.387 cm³ |
| 1 cu foot [ft³] | | 0.02832 m³ |
| 1 fluid ounce | 1.0408 UK fl oz | 29.574 ml |
| 1 pint (16 fl oz) | 0.8327 UK pt | 0.4732 litres |
| 1 gallon (231 in³) | 0.8327 UK gal | 3.7854 litres |

# Mass

| US or Imperial | | Metric |
|---|---|---|
| 1 ounce [oz] | 437.5 grain | 28.35 g |
| 1 pound [lb] | 16 oz | 0.4536 kg |
| 1 stone | 14 lb | 6.3503 kg |
| 1 hundredweight [cwt] | 112 lb | 50.802 kg |
| 1 short ton (US) | | 0.9072 t |

# THE WILD CAMEL PROTECTION FOUNDATION

In 1997, after John Hare's four pioneering trips on camels into the Gobi deserts of Mongolia and China where the wild camel survives, he and Kathryn Rae, an environmental lawyer, established the Wild Camel Protection Foundation (WCPF) as a UK registered charity Number 1068706. Thanks to a world-wide membership of over 700 people and energetic activities organised by Patrons, sufficient finance has been raised to accomplish an incredible amount of work to save the wild camel from extinction. In particular, a very successful wild camel breeding centre in Mongolia.

Increasing pressure by man on the remaining 1,000 wild camels' desert habitat, through influences such as illegal mining, means the future for the wild camel in both China and Mongolia is precarious. The announcement in 2008 that it is a **NEW and SEPARATE SPECIES of CAMEL** makes the work of the WCPF even more valuable and important. **WCPF is the only organization in the world with the sole aim of protecting the critically endangered wild camel from extinction.**

To become a member of WCPF please go to **www.wildcamels.com** or Email John Hare at **harecamel@aol.com**. Membership costs £20 ($25) per annum and members receive newsletters every year.

WCPF urgently needs funds for the establishment of a second wild camel breeding centre as the breeding centre at Zakhyn Us in Mongolia has reached its capacity of 30 wild camels. It was started in 2004 with just eight and now has 35, even though eight wild camels have been released into their natural habitat.

To raise these urgent funds, WCPF commissioned a portrait of a wild bull camel from Charlotte Williams who is a highly regarded wildlife artist with a fast-growing reputation. The portrait is entitled "The King of the Gobi" and is an excellent likeness and embodies all the resilient and stoical characteristics of the bull wild camel.

We have published a limited edition of 100 prints signed by the artist, 44 cms x 54 cms excluding border, and these are available for £200 (plus postage). To obtain a print please **email: harecamel@ aol.com** or go to the wild camel website: **www.wildcamels.com** where payment can be made via Paypal.

Jane Goodall DBE the Life Patron of the Wild Camel Protection Foundation has endorsed the portrait as can be seen from the photograph.

# Index

## General

# People

# Places

Moyale 30
Mugurr River 87
Northern Frontier District
    (NFD) 82
Nabayaton 88, 91
Nachurogwai Desert 83, 84
Nairobi 25, 27, 28, 45, 48, 78, 81
Nangurio River 42
Ol Maisor 4, 21, 25, 27, 29, 45,
76, 86, 91
Parkati 91
Porr 32
Rift Valley 3, 18, 90
Rumuruti 4
Sandy Bay 7, 25
Sibiloi  46, 47, 49, 53, 60, 76
Sirima Dry River 7, 25, 87, 91
South Horr 29
Suguta Nangal 87
Suguta Valley v, xii, 8, 9, 25, 27,
87, 88, 90
Tulu-gulas River 55
Turkana Basin 40
Turkwell River 11, 35, 57, 79
Lake Van, Turkey, 4
Libya 112

Tripoli 23, 112
Mongolia ix, xiii, 4, 33, 45, 85, 91,
    110
Niger 112
Nigeria x, 6, 33, 37, 112
  Bima Hill 93
  Gombe 92
  Jos 44
  Kukawa 23
  Lake Chad 112
  Mambilla Plateau 7, 111
  Mandara Mountains x
  Northern Nigeria 30, 33, 60, 84,
  111, 113
  Sengri, Alantika Mountains 92
  Tula, Tangale-Waja 33, 111
North Korea 60
Red Sea 90
Sahara desert 23, 37, 55
Sri Lanka 105
Somalia 30, 82
Sudan 110
Tanzania 9, 17, 75
  Mount Kilimanjaro 17
  Gombe National Park x
Uganda 38

# Tribes

Bodi 97, 100, 106, 107
Dassenech xii, 19, 42, 55, 56, 57,
    58, 59, 60, 61, 63, 65, 66, 67, 73,
    74, 97
El Molo 88, 89, 90
Gabbra 30, 31, 32, 41, 58, 59, 76,
    78, 80, 81, 117
Hamar 28, 97, 100
Hausa 113
Karo 97, 100
Kikuyu 13, 57
Koma 92
Kwegu 97, 100, 106, 107

Maasai 13, 62
Mursi 97, 100, 102, 106, 107
Oromo 31
Pokot [Suk] 20, 21, 83
Rendille 111
Samburu 19, 83,111
Somali 57, 116, 117
Turkana 8, 10, 19, 20, 21, 30, 32,
    38, 39, 42, 43, 55, 56, 58, 59, 63,
    65, 73, 76, 78, 79, 80, 82, 83, 86,
    89, 90, 91, 98, 111, 114, 115, 116